Common Ground

Common Ground

*Letters to a World
Community of Meditators*

Laurence Freeman

A Medio Media Book
Continuum • New York

1999
The Continuum Publishing Company
370 Lexington Avenue
New York, NY 10017

Printed in the United States of America.

Library of Congress Cataloging-in-Publication Data

Freeman, Laurence.
    Common ground : letters to a world community of meditators /
Laurence Freeman.
        p.   cm.
    ISBN 0-8264-1215-7 (pbk.)
    1. Meditation—Christianity.   I. Title
BV4813.F7   1999
248.3'4—dc21   99-31672
                                                                CIP

Contents

Introduction

On the threshold of the third millennium, the media are producing a spate of reviews of the world's history to date. A striking feature of these sweeping timelines is that human history seems so evidently a story of cruel conflict. The human inability to resolve differences deeply enough to prevent recurring eruptions of violence is our chronic failure to reconcile and forgive as all the great teachers of humanity have urged us to do.

Violence leads to violence; those who live by the sword will die by the sword. Human beings first heard that wisdom long ago, yet humanity continues in its addiction to patterns of ethnic cleansing, genocide, racial discrimination, and social exclusion. Religions have only recently begun to suspect that they are partners rather than competitors in breaking out of these patterns and creating a world where peace—sustainable peace—is the norm rather than an utopian ideal. Through dialogue, pilgrimage, and meditation together, the world faiths are just discovering that, without betraying their own unique and indispensable deposits of wisdom, they can also acknowledge a common ground. Standing together here in friendship—or better, perhaps, sitting on it together—the witness for peace will be undeniable and irresistible. In the last of the newsletters in this collection, there is a description of Buddhists and Christians sitting together on the common ground of the earth under the Bodhi tree in Bodhgaya, sacred as the site of the Buddha's enlightenment. Including this thirteenth letter in the book breaks the symmetry of the collections of twelve newsletters which began nearly twenty years ago. But it is a significant and beautiful enough event to make a new pattern for a new millennium.

Under the Bodhi tree, we meditated together. The common ground is contemplation: the silent, still, simple, non-disputational consciousness that we are essentially good and that the universe is friendly. Every faith tradition has its contemplative spirituality as well as its rites and dogma or philosophy, its scriptures and sacred places. By discovering the treasure of contemplative practice hidden in the field of our faiths, the common ground of humanity is brought into the open field of awareness.

These letters have already been circulated among a world-wide community of Christian meditators who are working each day at discovering this common ground in the depths of their own heart in their daily meditation periods and their contemplative way of living. The first step in finding the great common ground must be made within oneself and then with others in one's own community. The community which has grown directly out of practicing meditation together in the Christian tradition is one focused in faith and love in the person of Jesus rising from the dead. Because this experience of faith transforms the way we see each other, we are also able to explore the common ground shared equally with all other members of the human family, whether they are in the same family of faith or not.

It is as a community, therefore, that we now share more widely these letters that link us four times a year to a sense of a shared common path, vision, and adventure. Their themes are inspired by events within the life of the World Community for Christian Meditation, which also seems to have general relevance—a visit to prison, a seminar on Jesus, a gathering of Christian meditation teachers, a visit to a Buddhist master. As letters to family can do, they can sometimes ramble a bit, but we hope nonetheless that the news they bring is good.

I am very grateful again to Greg Ryan, the Community's webpage master and master networker. Each quarter, he prepares these letters for distribution worldwide by mail or the internet, and he has now helped to put them in shape for publication. I am also thankful to the amazing individuals, groups, and centres that form and reform this Community year by year and who have taught me whatever I have been able to share in these letters about the common ground which is humanity's hope and joy

Laurence Freeman, OSB

Letter One

14 December 1995

Holistic Community

Dearest friends,

In October, I gave a retreat at the Benedictine monastery in Pecos, New Mexico. It is a warm and friendly community seeking God through the monastic life, and their ministry of hospitality and prayer is inspired by the beauty of the surrounding mountains and desert. One evening, after the final meditation of the day, I walked to my room in a nearby building. The night was cold, and I did not want to linger. But as I looked up at the clear night sky over the desert, I was arrested by its overwhelming, silent grandeur. The Milky Way had never looked more like the pot of cream spilled over the universe by a careless cat as it is explained in some creation myths. I thought of how much we miss by living in cities under the constant artificial yellowy light which hides the beauties of the night.

Then I realized that I was still standing in the light cast from the building I had just left, and although it was not very bright, it was still reducing my view of the starlight. Stepping outside the pool of electric light was not difficult, but suddenly the desert looked very dark. The path I was standing on seemed very safe compared with the unknown land a few feet away. I remembered the warnings about rattlesnakes and the slithering sounds I had heard in the brush during my afternoon walk. Nevertheless, thinking that even snakes must sleep, I walked away from the light of the building and into the dark desert—not very far, but far enough to see the difference that the darkness made on my ability to see. There was no fear, only the grandeur of the universe speaking to one of its constituent specks of dust. I stayed until I remembered that I was cold.

Leaving the light of the mind for the darkness of faith makes us uneasy. When we sit to meditate, that is what we are doing—and the mind gives us many reasons for not doing it. There may be serpents in the deserted places, after all. We can, of course, see something of the sky of God from within the familiar pool of light cast by thought and imagination. So why risk more? Even if we move into the darkness of meditation, the new vision does not come immediately because it takes time for the eyes to adjust. Perseverance is demanding. But patience is a breeder reactor for faith. So what makes us take the step of faith? Surely it is nothing less than the grandeur, the glory, of God. The pure and simple attractiveness of God beside which the most powerful forces of human attraction must seem weak. There may be many reasons why we should not meditate; there is one overwhelming, delightful, and ultimately irresistible reason why we should.

All religious faith must lead us eventually to step off the familiar paths of the mind into the mystery of reality. Even simple reverence for human life would lead to it. In mystery—what we can know but not think—we discover the light that shines in the dark and which makes even the dark shine. It is more real than any other light. It has an inexhaustible power supply. Unless we are prepared to risk leaving our private worlds, how can we see the great world to which we truly belong and of which our little worlds are microcosms? Without leaving home, how can we discover that the cosmos is our true community?

The Christian Meditation Community in Australia had been going through some difficult times of internal tensions. When I arrived in September, I soon realized that these tensions tended toward growth and were hidden graces. The national community of meditators had grown steadily over the past ten years, both in depth of consciousness and in organization. So there were simple human laws of development being enacted as they must be in any group. Conflict, as St Benedict well knew, is an integral part of community and personal growth. Even the cosmic community of molecules, animals, and humans, on earth and far into the night sky, interact, disagree, and pull in differing directions before achieving a higher synthesis of identity and form.

What matters is not avoiding conflict but resolving it with courage born of the love which impels all transcendence, all growth. The grace for me with the Australian meditators was to share in their love and openness to change. On retreat and also in dialogue together, the Spirit was sensibly present and leading them not only to a new form of the community, but also to a new energy of hope and generosity in their work of sharing their gift with others.

John Main believed deeply that meditation creates, reveals, and realizes community. He did not say that it removes the challenge of community or makes it easy. Meditation highlights community as a basic aspect of all reality—our bodies, our bodies and minds, our personal and social relationships, our links to earth and cosmic forces are all communities within communities. Community is reality and not just a way of escaping the cosmos, ourselves, or others, or of making a base for our own self-fulfillment. Despite the glib ways we use the term *community* today, meditation restores us to its basic meaning. To be in *comm-unity* is to be with oneness. Our modern search for community is in direct proportion to our nightmare experience of isolation and social fragmentation.

In the *Prologue to the Rule,* St Benedict says that God seeks his labourer in the multitude and asks who wants life. God calls him out of the crowd by the great mind-opening question of life—do you really want to be alive? If you say yes, you are led from the anonymity of the crowd into community. Here you are given support and help from others who are also seeking. You will be tested as they are and will be tempted to revert to the alienated state of the multitude. The early monks took themselves off to the desert, and we *today* must find the pregnant emptiness within ourselves. Whatever the form of the call to community—St Benedict says there are many kinds of monks and Celtic monasteries even included the married—we must first respond to it. It is heard, somehow, somewhere, beyond ordinary mental hearing and perhaps beyond ordinary mental time. Once heard, though, it lifts us up out of one life, and we find ourselves, despite our fears, on a new path.

A recent survey in the United States showed how extreme our modern individualism and alienation are becoming. It showed how different individualism is from individuation—isolation from finding our true self. The survey showed a dramatic shrinking of membership rolls in every kind of association from the Elks to the Boy Scouts, church attendance to bowling leagues, PTAs to political groups. In a related question, people in 1960 generally agreed that most people can be trusted; while today, only a third of those questioned trust others. Community is place of trust—we know we are in it together. In the crowd, we compete, we threaten, and we trust no one absolutely. Crowds breed misery. When we are isolated and frightened of dying alone, we are too scared of ourselves to step outside the pool of artificial light into the dark majesty which glows with the whole reality of life and its meaning. The bigger our cities, the more lights we burn at night—lights that are visible to astronauts but which keep us in the dark.

All growth proceeds toward fullness through stages. Natural growth can be helped or hindered but not fundamentally controlled, although biology today is changing our definitions of all these things. We grow in community, beyond one form into another. Community itself is our context of growth and our path for seeking God. Its stages demand patience, acceptance, and reverence for those with whom we share this particular form of community.

The first stage is the call from the crowd. Our education and society should help create the conditions that allow it to be heard by each person. Because if we cannot hear the call, how can we respond? Religion and society are meant to sharpen our hearing, heighten our expectation, rather than drown out the unique call God addresses to each of us with their own ideologies or dogma. So, with the help of our first teachers, we hear our own name being called, and we disengage ourselves from the crowd mentality. The silent utterance of our own name is redemptive. It opened the mind of Mary Magdalene to recognize the risen Jesus. For us today, enmeshed in the addictive processes of a consumer culture and blinded by economic goals, meditation allows us the space to grow and the silence to hear who God is telling us we truly are. Once this call is heard, our personal history of salvation and enlightenment has begun.

If the call leads us into an organized form of community, its organized structure should not act like a crowd. The institutional structure of the church, for example, should not oppress the communal nature of its membership which is its true identity. Communities can quickly degenerate into crowds, especially when leadership ceases to be prophetic. Religious communities that have in fact become crowds—wolves in sheep's clothing—serve only to drown out the sacred hearing of one's own name spoken by God. Then those persons who do hear their call often find themselves turned on by the community.

So much discretion is needed in community, to balance structure and liberty, that St Benedict realized that rules for community can only be guidelines rather than laws. As the best desert fathers also taught, we learn best by example, not coercion. Nevertheless, in this first stage of leaving the crowd and entering the communal mode of consciousness, we need to be humble enough to listen to a voice other than our own ego. To learn this, we must learn the spiritual meaning of obedience and discipline.

A second stage unfolds as we persevere in this new way of living in community, a way of living with an awareness of relationship and interdependence in all areas of life. This is where the sparks start flying. The closer we come to losing our self-centredness, the stronger are the forces of egocentric gravity pulling us back into a self-centred orbit controlled by the polarities of fear and desire. Marriages, monastic vows, and any serious life-commitment or undertaking demand the same community-based responses of fidelity and mutual obedience. At this stage, we quickly face the paradox of resisting what we most desire. At this stage, we easily rationalize our fears and project our faults onto others. Modern people slip into psycho-speech which often thinly veils judgementalism and condemnation of others from an assumed ledge of psychological superiority. We are quick to point out others' projections, but we are less sharp-eyed in seeing our own.

Community teaches us that the ego cannot be crushed out of existence. It can be battered, bruised, and deformed, but it is amazingly resilient. If we try—as earlier religious approaches did—to destroy the ego, we merely become dysfunctional and unhealthy in normal life, and our normal drives, personal or social, become distorted. The ego is necessary, in a healthy state, for the making of relationships as well as for the practicalities of life. It is the necessary fuel of transcendence. It takes a healthy ego, for example, to drive in heavy traffic without becoming demonic! Jesus taught that the true self is the source of all value and meaning in life. We seek it in our seeking of God, and we inevitably confront the inner dynamics of fear and the patterns of projection which block us from communion with self and others. At those times, everything depends on whether we persevere with the seeking or collapse into the patterns of fear and projection. We can take flight from the quest by blaming either ourselves or others for failure, for being unbalanced or unjust. Or we can blame God. The paradox of community is that we need the support of others if we are to overcome our natural resistance to being one with them. Redemption flows from this paradox. Our deepest need for community is addressed by the birth of God as a human being.

The miracle is the unfailingly faithful love available to us. From somewhere we cannot observe or control, there issues an intelligent, subtle guidance of infinite patience and unlimited forgiveness. It is in community that we can most often perceive the invisible movements of the Holy Spirit. The root of the word *meditation* is the same as that of *medicine*. It suggests exactly what the Advocate does: the work of curing, caring, healing, and making whole. Meditation is crucial for all the deeper levels of relationship precisely because it is there that we meet the hidden sources of fear and negation at work within our own minds.

As we become familiar with the struggle between ego-centredness and other-centredness through the life of community, we stumble across solitude. The ego often seeks withdrawal and isolation, but this is false solitude. Real solitude is the acceptance of our absolute uniqueness. Everything capable of saying "I" is cosmically unique—although Simone Weil said that only God has the right to say "I." In solitude, we recognize and accept this uniqueness which is imperceptible in the crowd. Through entering the next stage of community which is solitude, we may discover what the crowd could never teach—our capacity to be alone and to avoid distraction. Lifestyles change as a result. We may no longer observe our ritual four hours of television each day. In conflict with others, we are less reactive and wiser in waiting. The essence of solitude is not physical isolation, but inner silence and the capacity to rest in situations without judgment. It is the opposite of isolation as the community is the reverse of the crowd.

The meditation group is a good example of this. When we meditate together, we are, like Jesus in the gospel, "praying alone in the presence of our friends"—solitary and in community. So the weekly group strengthens and refreshes us for the daily practise. Members of the group do not meet for entertainment, novelty, or social chat but to celebrate the sacrament of basic community: the more ordinary, the more real, and the more nourishing. The weekly meditation community bears fruit in family life and work as well as in the more intimate depths of our being.

The ultimate community is God. Our experience of oneness at any level is a participation in the divine mystery of life. What holds us together—in every sense—is God.

Solitude is, therefore, the work of community and is arrived at through community. Those who can be solitary are capable of true friendship, and it is in friendship that Christian spirituality finds its meaning. When Jesus called his disciples servants no longer but friends, it was because he had revealed to them all that he had learned. This declaration of friendship transforms the way we can conceive of the master-disciple relationship and, indeed, our relationship with God. It summons us to a progressive journey into the experience of community through the interwoven dimensions of personal wholeness, human relationship, Christ, and God. In the end, God is all in all—St Paul's great holistic statement and vision. Christianity has this inclusiveness at the heart of its mission. It can ill afford to relapse into exclusivist, cultist status.

Friendship is perhaps the best human model we have to describe how divergent traditions and faiths can converge without betraying their precious, sacred uniqueness. In ancient cultures, friendship was regarded as the highest achievement of human relationships. Today we speak of being just friends. Yet friendship is the way the Holy Spirit manifests itself to us as the bond of that community which constitutes the nature of God. God is the primordial community. The harmony of the universe is the expression of this divine community, from the manner in which atoms make molecules and humans make friends. Christ is the sacrament of this unity and the catalyst of ultimate reunion with the Source. So to make friends with one another and friends with our enemies, to treasure tolerance and respect our differences must be the goal of all religion.

Only solitude can provide the depth for such universal friendship. Those who can be solitary have withdrawn their projections and are innately nonviolent. They have broken with the crowd, and their communities do not become rival crowds in their turn. Solitude gives us the transformational insight that all things are held together in the boundless, open community of God. To be friends with one another then is only seeing that we are in God together. This insight is the criterion of all genuine human holiness. It was and is the experience of Christ.

Be holy as I am holy. (Lev 11:44)

This is the human vocation in the biblical vision. Yet holiness sounds rather boring today. It has become so identified with religious people being religious and conforming to their own rules and conventions that, as a term, it has become ghettoized. For many people outside organized religion, holiness can even sound hypocritical. After all, if holiness means conformity, then it is a small step to thinking that conforming superficially is better than not conforming at all. This kind of convention-driven holiness convinces fewer and fewer people today.

Yet the most vibrant movements in modern spirituality are holistic—integrating body and mind, self with others, humanity with nature. Many of these movements have their own flaws and even take on the faults of organized religion, but they often better reflect the real aspiration to holiness which bestows meaning on life. However, the main religious traditions have the power to remind us to seek holiness within the whole, not just as a private experience. They return us to the sense of the sacred in all things, and it is this insight into natural holiness which radiates in the Bible. In Eden, everything was holy, including the body and all its contacts with the world. After that fragmentation of consciousness that we call the Fall, the sense of the sacred was also splintered. Religion attempts to reintegrate it. Thus, religion sees places and clothes, days and seasons, altars, oils, and the musical instruments used in worship as holy. Ordinary things dedicated to transcendence become holy and sources of holiness. Above all, the people are holy in the Bible, and they participate in the holiness of the One who alone, as Jesus said, is good.

Every culture has its purity maps and regulations which it obliges its members to respect. Certain people (AIDS sufferers perhaps, immigrants, or in biblical terms, lepers or tax-gatherers) can be designated unclean and, therefore, unholy. Certain foods, practises, states of the body are similarly mapped. Regulations governing these maps try to preserve the holiness of the righteous by separating them from the unholy. But we can only be holy by being one with the whole and absorbing the unholy into the holy. Thus, holiness involves transgressing into the unholy, the profane. Jesus touched lepers, ate with sinners, and conversed with single women. He opened the kingdom to foreigners. Because he was holy, he could not respect what denied human wholeness, and he stepped off his culture's own purity map.

Holiness demands courage, the courage born of solitude. Until that courage is born in us, we cannot reach the goal for which we thirst and strive for most deeply. Until we are conscious that we participate by right in the community of God and God's universe, we can enjoy no great *shalom*. Obedience to religious rules and conventions are not manifestations of holiness in themselves. They are preparations for an experience which unfolds in life and in relationships, which expresses itself above all in compassion and unlimited friendship. In itself, it is the opening of the eye of the heart. It removes the film of ignorance which clouds insight into the true nature of reality.

"We shall be like him because we shall see him as he is" (1 Jn 3:2). We grow in holiness through seeing, through insight. Recently, I was helped in understanding the nature of insight during a presentation by John Little, one of the Australian meditation community coordinators. John is a business management consultant, and his thinking has been influenced of late by the philosophy of Bernard Lonergan, whose great book *Insight* is a study of human understanding. Lonergan argues that understanding is more than just looking at or even thinking about something. It is a process of many acts which culminate in insight. John Little was talking about these ideas in relation to the decision-making process to a high-powered group of business and government people.

At just the right moment in his talk, he then handed out a number of puzzles on which to test their own experience of insight. One asked how to put ten smarties into three cups so that an odd number was in each cup. The group entered into the puzzles with enthusiasm, but then as they found them to be more difficult than they had imagined, their reactions changed. Some struggled not to show the frustration and anger which were aroused. Others betrayed their sense of failure and inferiority. When insight is blocked or has not yet come, these deep emotions can surface suddenly and affect the environment. If the insight comes, it comes less as a result of thinking and analysis. It bubbles up intuitively as it did for Archimedes when he got into the bath at his Eureka! moment or as with many modern scientists who come to their greatest discoveries in dream or day-dream states.

When insight dawns, we feel relief, exultation, and delight. Sheer joy. Then, in the lesser insights arising from the lesser puzzles of life, such as how to put smarties into cups, we have to check the insight and integrate it. Holiness grows through insights at all levels of our life and consciousness. But it is deepened by the fundamental insight which happens when we see through ourselves. This comes when the brick wall of the ego and the naked awareness of self yield to the mind of Christ. Our isolated individuality, with its inherent sorrow, expands to reveal true individuation, showing that we are indivisible parts of the great whole. Egotistic fixation on our own sinfulness or on the sins of others is absorbed in the perception of God as all in all.

These stages of realizing community and our essential holiness are each a kind of rebirth. Christmas places human birth at the heart of our relationship to God. It teaches us that our life's births are not isolated events, loose ends, but parts of a single great birth. Just as there is one community—God—of which all communities are expressions, so all births express the begetting of the Son in the heart of the Godhead. The birth of Jesus of Nazareth is our birth. It brings into time the birth of the eternal Word from the Ground of Being. From that comes the birth of the cosmos with all its beauties and mysteries. And finally, our own human birth, unique and precious and the beginning of a slow awakening to who we are, where we have come from, and where we are going.

The weeks of the Christmas season should remind us of original unity. The birth of Jesus, as of every human child, confronts us with the power of innocence and simplicity—a power most of us see diminish as we develop until a certain stage of our journey recalls us to it at a higher level. Christmas reminds us of the simplicity of God and of the universe, beside which our own complexities are suddenly resolved. It chases away fear and reaffirms the holiness of the life we have been given and that we are. And the humanity of God in Jesus makes us feel once again the wonder of being human, the privilege of having been born.

It has been a great happiness to me in the recent months of traveling to see the community and wholeness evident in so many of our fellow meditators around the world. This community is one of the signs of God's presence in the modern world which we should cherish and celebrate as a source of hope and inspiration for the future. May we all be strengthened and made happy by this. And may the peace and joy of Jesus, whose love flows in unbroken, moving stillness throughout the universe and through our own lives, heal, renew, and teach us what he wishes us to see.

With much love

Laurence

Laurence Freeman, OSB

Information, discussion forums, and photos of John Main and the Meditation Community may be viewed at the WCCM web site: www.wccm.org.

Letter Two

21 March 1996
Feast of Saint Benedict

Unblocking Love

Dearest friends,

Over the past few months, during which I have been concentrating on writing—*sitting* and writing—I have had the opportunity to reflect on the distinction between stillness and stiffness. A few hours of sitting at a table accumulates an unexpected karma of stiffness. If you are not naturally athletic and do not rid yourself of the stiffness immediately, it builds up over the days until the body's lack of suppleness reflects itself in a loss of mental subtlety. Eventually, you stretch—delightfully, if a little painfully. Blocked energy is released, and new energy, together with a new harmony of body and mind, is recreated. Having shaken off the stiffness, you find you can sit still again.

I was reminded of this while listening to a talk by Father John in the *Communitas* series in which he responded to a question about what was the best way to prepare for a period of meditation. You might have expected him to say by reading scripture, listening to music, or maybe even stretching. Instead, he said, "perform small acts of kindness during the day." From our own experience, we know how these quiet, unobtrusive, often unnoticeable gestures of love can make or break a day. They are a kind of spiritual exercise, dispelling the darkness that can thicken the mind over time and releasing the stiffness, the blocked energy of love caused by egotism.

We can easily get stuck in the same position of self-centredness. Only gradually do we realize why we are so emotionally and mentally stiff. As soon as we can notice that we are hurt whenever we are forced to turn away from ourselves, we are in possession of a great grace. Coming into a spiritual practise which allows us to stretch regularly—all exercise, like meditation, should be steady, moderate, and regular—is just such a grace.

Small acts of kindness, as Father John suggested, do much to make for the truly "good life." But, of course, it is the way we perform them that really counts. Jesus speaks about good deeds which we like other people to see us performing and applaud at. Such acts stroke the ego. There is no virtuous deed, whatever it may cost us, which cannot be such an egotrap. In the spiritual laboratory of their desert, the early monks practised their good deeds of chastity, fasting, solitude, and self-control; yet they realized that a perfect performance could hide a terrible hypocrisy. All virtuous action can be a minefield of pride and self-congratulation. The only hope and our best guide is, as the Desert Christians knew, humility.

Jesus said that the left hand must not know what the right is doing when we perform our small acts of kindness. In other words, we must learn to be humble in everything we do. Genuine purity of heart is unselfconscious—and so, the less said about it, the better! Best of all, though, is when we surprise ourselves by realising retrospectively that we did something kind without thinking about it. When one hand knows what the other is doing, we risk exploiting others by our very acts of kindness toward them.

The mantra is a great teacher of humility and kindness. With practise, we learn to say it unselfconsciously, and this develops a diminishing egotism, a healthier ego, in daily life. The small acts of kindness that prepare us for meditation may be a smile to a tired supermarket clerk or an act of elementary politeness to a friend. They prepare us for the time of the mantra, but they are also performed on the wave of energy which the mantra helps to release. The mantra itself is a small act of kindness, bringing us to unselfconscious self-knowledge. It helps us to love ourselves, so that we can love others. If we cannot be kind to ourselves, it is unlikely we will ever be nice to others. Done in secret, as Jesus recommended all good deeds should be, the mantra sounds silently through every thought, word, and deed of our life.

Shaking off my stiffness one day, I found myself before the deep stillness of Monet's water lilies. These are vast canvases of colour inspired by his beloved garden at Giverny: colour and texture capturing the delicate, evanescent personality of the flowers and the still water on which they float in their own quiet reflection. From past experience, I knew that to find yourself in that extraordinarily alive stillness which Monet had captured—or released—in his paintings demanded time. When you walk into the gallery, as when you go to church or to your usual meditation place, your mind is careering around in its hundred thousand things. Many visitors came through the room, caught the paintings on their camcorders, and shot off briskly to another experience. A few sat in the room waiting for their own stillness to meet the stillness of the water lilies.

The depth of stillness which art can create is spiritual rather than religious. But it can inspire the same reverence and wonder by arousing through the senses the awareness of the sacred in the ordinary. Yet the water lilies had no story to tell, no before or after. Everything on the wide canvas was simultaneously present. There was no attempt to define. Only a wonder in being.

Meditation is an art of prayer which we all, even the most untalented, can do. Like every art, it needs practise and discipline, and it rewards us with truth, beauty, and an insight into the essential goodness of being. Monet painted what he saw, without pretence and without imposing his theories on what he saw. Some of his fellow Impressionists, who were ridiculed and rejected by the art establishment of their day, sacrificed a great deal for this purity of heart. Many were so poor that they painted on newspapers and reused the same canvas many times in order to practise their art. Like them, meditators are poor artists, less interested in the rewards than in doing their work with integrity. Any riches or experiences that come to them are purely accidental, sheer gift.

The difference between art and prayer is that art is always in some way a reflected image, while prayer is a total union of image and reality. The beauty of prayer is that we are the image of God becoming fully alive with the glory of God. If there is a reflection of this, it is in the small and great acts of kindness by which we relate to one another, mirroring God in each other's souls and daily lives. It is all one work—meditation and love. So it is really unnecessary to make a great fuss about analysing the experience, separating life and prayer, or even preparing for the stillness.

Monet's stillness is moving—so moving because it awakens the depth of consciousness where prayer is constantly flowing in us without a ripple—a stillness that is pure liberty. The mantra might be compared to the brush which responds to this indwelling still-ness at the heart of all life and draws it into conscious experience. Saying the mantra, like applying the brush, is much more than a technique. It is an act which deftly concentrates the whole person in a single point of unity. It comes from a centred poise of atten-tion—rather than a pose looking for attention.

Everything comes into being by the utterance of the Word of God. The mantra, like every word, is a creative act. Many people are understandably frightened of speaking because they know that when they speak they have done something which has irreversible consequences. It is wise, then, to think before you speak. It is wiser still to meditate before you think.

Our fear of self-expression is partly based on the awareness that words can often convey what we would prefer them not to. Self-expression can become self-revelation. If our words unconsciously convey anger, prejudice, fear, illusion, or any of our other demons, they leave a bitter repentance behind them. Meditation restores our confidence in words as acts that can convey kindness and truth. It makes us more free to communicate because its goal is the pure, simple, and wholly truthful saying of a single word. If we can say one word truthfully, we come closer to the goal of that pure speech which made the words of Jesus "spirit and life."

The mantra is a word of God and to say it simply and to listen to it selflessly realises perfect communication. This is Spirit—the pure, unbounded, and undistorted communication within the Trinity of Love that is God. When communication is perfect, no more words are necessary. The pure word leads into silence.

Nor is this just a peak experience, like the silence on a mountain top. It is with us continuously. Silence, like the stillness of medita-tion, allows us to speak truthfully in everyday conversation, to avoid the untruths of gossip and condemnation in which we indulge so readily and so self-deceptively. We replace this counter-feit currency with the true coin of kindness. From the work of silence in meditation each day, we emerge better prepared to speak the truth more simply and accurately, to know what we want to say, what we should not say, and what we can say. This is discretion: one of the gifts of the Holy Spirit, a fruit of silence, and the practical exercise of compassion in human affairs.

The silent word of the mantra sounds at the centre of consciousness even while we are speaking or acting. It helps to keep us stabilised when strong emotions flare up. And when we have lost balance, meditation restores us to it quickly. Modern life is so alienated from the ordinary human qualities of balance, harmony, and contentment that we often hunger for them with the aching desire we feel for unrealisable ideals. The ordinary witness of daily meditators over time is that these human qualities are realistic possibilities. Even the anxiety we feel at the prospect of being free of our anxieties can be calmed by a steady and unselfconscious practise of silence.

The simplicity and humility of the mantra help us to avoid or, at least, to recognise the pitfalls of pride and possessiveness. The mantra teaches us, for example, that good as harmony, balance, and contentment are, they cannot be objects of desire or states to which we should cling. Yet they are worth striving for because they allow us to remain in continuous communication, open to the spirit of truth even in the valleys of suffering or the plateaux of discouragement. The mantra sounds equally in the peaks and valleys of the soul as well as up the mountain slopes of life. It helps to give a unity to all experience. If meditation helps us to grow, it is because growth means the coming together of the high and the low, the inner and the outer dimensions of life.

Well, (people often say) this may all be true, but why put so much emphasis on the mantra? Surely, we can come to silence without saying a word all the time. And if we are concentrating on the mantra, aren't we actually distracting ourselves from what God might be saying to us?

I think you will only persevere in meditation if you really want to. And you will only want to if you understand what it is really about. You will only understand it fully by practising it regularly. I once knew a man who meditated valiantly for a couple of years just to please his wife. When he was advised to cut down on his many activities and take a sabbatical from his good works, to slow down, the first thing he thankfully abandoned was meditation! Unless your practise leads you to understand for yourself why the mantra is not a distraction and how it leads to ever deeper silence, the best of teachers will be of no use.

Why say the mantra at all? A man and his friend were once taking goods to market on a donkey. At night, they stopped, and the friend was concerned to secure the donkey. He was surprised to see its owner wave his hands around the donkey's feet as if tying them. The donkey, thinking it was tied, did not move all night. In the morning when the friend tried to get the donkey going, it still refused to move. The owner came and again waved his hands around the donkey's feet as if untying it. Convinced now that it was free, the donkey trotted happily off. One illusion was needed to dispel another.

If we try to let go by an act of the will, we end by clinging even tighter. If we make an effort to be spontaneous, we become more self-conscious. Similarly, if we try to still the mind by thinking about stilling the mind, then the mind spins faster than ever. We need a deceptively simple way to achieve what, in fact, cannot be achieved at all, only realised or awakened.

Does this mean that the mantra is just a technique? It could, of course, be practised as a technique, to achieve desired ends such as relaxation, lowering blood-pressure, or improving exam results. But when it is practised every day, twice a day, regardless of the weather (as it is when it is part of the Way of Christian faith or other spiritual traditions), meditation transcends technique. It becomes over time an act of discipleship, a simple act of kindness and reverence toward our teacher, who is both our lord and friend. Our faith at this point makes it easier to understand why the mantra is a discipline.

All discipleship aims at the superseding of the ego. The disciplines of discipleship help the ego to evolve to its next stage of development.

The birth of the ego as a part of human consciousness is evocatively painted in the biblical myth of the Fall of Adam and Eve, which Catholics read at mass on the second Sunday of Lent. The story tells of the terrible awakening to self-consciousness we all pass through as we taste the difference between good and evil. Necessary at this stage within the general evolution of consciousness, it produces painful by-products of anxiety and shame. "Who told you you were naked?" the Creator asks the fallen Adam who had already begun to hide from him. The birth of the ego sets an irreversible course for each person, making it impossible for them to return to the Eden of their pre-conscious innocence. As the Bible goes on poignantly to say, henceforth, work is hard, and our birth into the world is the beginning of suffering.

The gospel of the same mass describes the temptation of Jesus in the desert. Led by the Spirit into the forty day fast that prepares him for his mission, Jesus endures the repeated onslaughts of the ego. He faces its demonic pride and the raging desire for self-sufficiency and supremacy. Jesus confronts the dark forces of his humanity, and by remaining still under their attack, all of humanity enjoys a share in his breakthrough. In Jesus, humanity takes its next great evolutionary step: the transcendence of the ego. Contemplating and sharing in his example, we learn to move beyond egotism to true selfhood and to a mature knowledge of God.

Meditation is, at times, the desert of our encounter with egotism. While we are there, fasting is our strength. We fast from all that the ego so readily uses for its claims and pretensions: thoughts, images, desires, plans, judgements, and anxieties. Such a fast, as Jesus taught, need not and should not be a depressing or mournful experience. It is not a self-inflicted punishment or even a reparation for earlier mistakes. It is a preparation for the movement of grace which sweeps us up and onward beyond the birth of the ego to its integration and transcendence.

Fasting from food can slow us down. Less energy is wasted. Action and thought become clearer, more economical. In the same way, in the fast of meditation, we learn to say the mantra without haste or unnecessary effort. Care, attention, clarity, and quality of consciousness replace impatience and distraction. At first, the mind does hurry and says the mantra as it runs. Later, as the centre of consciousness moves to the heart, we say the mantra more slowly, more deeply, and with the subtler rhythms of the spirit. As the present moment grows to be a stronger reality—in our meditation and in daily life—we worry less about time and pay more attention to the here and now.

Attention to detail, like the small acts of kindness which prepare us for meditation itself, characterise the pilgrimage of the mantra.

When you prepare a room for an honoured guest staying with you, you take trouble to clean it thoroughly, to make it attractive, and give more than ordinary attention to the details of its furnishing. In a similar way, saying the mantra is a detailed work—precise, small, and ordinary, and in its way, it is also a work of hospitality. But the more attention we give the work of the mantra, the more it becomes a work of universal significance. In saying it, we permit the spirit of Jesus to fill and, as he says, to complete us. We transfer the attention usually paid egotistically to ourselves to another, to *the* Other whom we can never know as an object outside ourselves.

From the desert of fasting, Jesus accompanies us to the Mount of Transfiguration. There, even before death, we can taste the first fruits of the Resurrection. Each of these milestones on the pilgrimage of the human spirit, and all the points between, are dimensions of the daily experience of prayer. We live the gospel events of Jesus' life in our own experience and come to understand their meaning through him. In this way, prayer fills ordinary life with an extraordinary wonder.

To deepen our commitment to prayer is one of the meanings and purposes of Lent which prepares us for a more powerful celebration of Easter's mysteries. Deepening commitment, however, does not mean merely adding more prayers or even more time for prayer. It is to purify prayer. By practising a little more daily mindfulness and self-control, guarding our eyes and ears a little more attentively, for example, we inevitably become a little less distracted and egocentric at the regular times of prayer. The advice of the early teachers was to practise the state in which you wish to rest in prayer between the times of prayer. Just remembering that "it is Lent" at odd moments of the day helps toward this. And as St Benedict suggests to the meditator in his Rule for monks, life is, in this sense, a continuous Lent.

This serves to strengthen our understanding of meditation as "pure prayer." By this traditional term, John Main meant that it is the way into the prayer practised continuously, in the present moment of the spirit, by Jesus. And Jesus himself reveals this when he tells us to "pray in my name." If that were to mean a magical incantation or a wish-fulfilling spell, then it could not also be the "worship in spirit and truth," for which, he says, humanity has now become ready. "The time is coming, indeed it is already here, when true worshippers will worship in spirit and in truth." And yet Jesus says, all our desires are fulfilled when we pray "in his name."

By saying this, Jesus acknowledges the reality of our needs and desires. We carry them with us like baggage on every journey we make, at every moment of the day. Even when they are unconscious, they control us from the wings. Unfulfilled desire is like heavy baggage, and there is nothing worse than travelling with heavy bags. They tie you down, add labour to every small decision. Fulfilled desires, however, only lighten the load a little and do so temporarily. Soon we acquire more souvenirs, and the bags get heavy again. Only radical freedom from desire *en-lightens* the spirit entirely. When we meditate, we try to take only carry-on baggage with us and then to divest ourselves even of that as soon as possible.

Jesus tells us that when we see him again in the Resurrection, we will have nothing more to ask him. By then, we will have been set free from desire. In the meantime, all our needs will be prayed in his name. This is from an Aramaic phrase, *beshemi,* which means "in my way," "with my understanding," or "according to my method or approach." Praying in this way, we receive whatever we ask for and our joy is thus made complete.

But do we ask for anything when we meditate? Certainly we do. We *ask* purely, simply, and without desire, images, or words. We ask for nothing. We ask for everything. In response, we receive the fullness of joy. This is what it means to ask in faith. Every other way of asking offers my will as an alternative to the divine will or attempts to negotiate with God.

The more we can let go of possessions and desires, the more we are free to enjoy what we are being given moment by moment. To our surprise, we may discover that we can enjoy even what we first found undesirable. So, the mantra is a way of praying "in his name." It permits us, as he did, to turn our attention wholly away from our self-centred mind and toward the Spirit and its pure, unconditional, and boundless joy.

It takes time to be with the present moment *as it is.* Sometimes, a long time. A friend told me recently of a visit she made out of curiosity to a casino in Las Vegas. As she arrived, a bus drew up and began to unload a group of elderly people. Most of them needed help to walk into the building, and some even had oxygen support on their wheelchairs. She watched them head for their favourite gambling spots and begin their session of steely-eyed, joyless compulsion. If there is one thing sadder than a prematurely aged child, it is the immaturity and the unripeness of the old. In both cases, time has been abused. It takes time. And time is so precious that we cannot afford to waste it. The irony of our culture is that it regards one of the best uses we can put time to—meditation—as the greatest waste of time.

It takes time to meditate—about two half-hours a day, for example. And time is needed to unknot the deep-set patterns of mind that hold us locked into certain feelings and types of behaviour. We even need time to be freed from the anxiety that arises when we see the prospect of being free from anxiety. Facing the illusory need to be addicted, living from an image rather than the reality of our self: this is what makes meditation a work rather than an indulgence. At the beginning, it is hard work. It becomes less hard once we have begun. But how long does it take us to begin? Maybe ten years pass before we realise that there is no turning back, and that once we have put our hand to the plough, we should not even look back. We *cannot* even look back. We have not really begun until we know that we are always beginning. We can say we have begun when we know the only direction is onward. We have really begun when we are doing it simply every day.

It is not easy in our culture to keep the great liturgical seasons very reverently. Santa Claus appears with the fall sales in the department stores, and chocolate bunnies fill the supermarkets from Ash Wednesday on! But I hope Lent has been a time of peaceful preparation for you, and Easter will again surprise you with its joy.

To deepen our saying of the mantra is the best way to understand what meditation means. And if we are meditating, the significance of these ancient spiritual cycles, which link the inner and outer seasons, must also deepen. In prayer, we pass through every season, birth, life, and death, and we can see their meaning because all these are enlightened by Resurrection.

To sit still is to shed the stiffness of egotism. To practise the discipline of prayer as a disciple is to be released from self-consciousness and to grow in spontaneity and innocence. The mantra is a small act of kindness, both to ourselves and to the world. It is a brushstroke of stillness, a look of pure attention, a joyful fast, a way of praying in the name of Jesus. It is one of the many things we can celebrate when we remind ourselves, each other, and the world that the ego and even death is transcended because—Alleluia—Christ is risen.

With much love

Laurence

Laurence Freeman, OSB

Letter Three
8 June 1996
The Cloud of Unknowing

Dearest friends,

I have been spending a lot of time with *The Cloud of Unknowing* recently, working on an introduction for a new edition. This little book, written five hundred years ago in war-torn, plague-devastated England while the papacy in Rome had been split in two and the peasant classes were rising against the landowners, speaks also to us in our troubled era about the way of mindfulness and the way to peace.

We have to make historical allowances while reading it, of course. For one thing, the author would have been surprised, perhaps shocked, to think of popular paperbacks of his book in mass circulation. His concept of contemplation was still highly restrictive. Written as a letter to a young monk encouraging him to enter and persevere in the form of cloistered religious life called "contemplative," the book sees this form of life as a higher stage than the ordinary, active life of most people. He could not have imagined the way the contemplative tradition would spill out from the cloister in modern times and turn his hierarchical "Holy Church" into a contemplative church of the laity. But I do not think he would have objected; in fact, the active and contemplative dimensions of life, in his view, subtly shade into each other.

He knew that the sign of the call to contemplation was the longing for it. It is this that he is responding to in his young friend. Contemplation itself, he said, bore fruit in the lives of the living and of the dead, and so it could never be said to be inactive. He would have seen that the work of love which united the soul to God could not exclude any type of person, anywhere.

A train of thought connected with this was started by an incident during my recent trip to Texas. One evening, I had just arrived and settled in where I was staying when I went for a walk, hoping to find a store in order to buy some toothpaste. Dusk was falling, and the sidewalks were empty. Only the late commuter traffic rushed past. There was no store in sight. As I crossed a church parking lot, I saw someone walking toward me, and with a stranger's innocence, I asked him, a black man, if there was a store nearby. When I saw how surprised he was by my speaking to him, I realised what a gulf I had crossed in speaking to him. I began to fear what he seemed surprised that I did not fear. He recovered before I did and then told me that there was no store nearby. I thanked him and turned away, but he called me back and offered to drive me to one. I was torn between admiration of American generosity and imagining the announcement at the retreat the next day mourning my tragic disappearance.

It was one of those moments of decision that seem to stop time and that are filled with an equal potential for fear and love, courage and despair. A moment of mindfulness. The kindness of strangers often propels us into those moments as if they are an unpredictable encounter with intervening grace, like the angelic visitors of the Bible. I am glad to say I accepted his offer. In chatting with him on the way, I learned he had moved to that part of town because crime was less there. I wondered if he had been frightened that I was going to mug him. And I found my toothpaste.

When I next read *The Cloud*, I found myself thinking of that incident in the light of a particular passage. *The Cloud* urges the reader to persevere in this work faithfully "until it becomes your whole life." It seemed to me that it must mean that the work of love would only reach its goal when it filled your whole being and so became your completely intuitive and spontaneous response to every situation in life. And perfect love casts out fear. The meditator should be fearless. The goal of the contemplative life is not to withdraw from the world of strangers. It is fulfilled only when in every stranger, one recognises not the projection of one's prejudices or fears, not a stereotype, but a unique manifestation of the divine.

Mindfulness is not an isolating objectification of reality. It is not a way of looking at a screen in front of us. The detachment of mindfulness brings us closer, into oneness, with ordinary reality. The monk or meditator, according to one of the desert fathers, is detached from all and in union with all. She sees herself in others and others in herself. When this state of mindfulness with others is realised, then the soul, in the words of *The Cloud*, is also "oned with God." We cannot love the God we cannot see if we do not love the stranger we do see. In fact, our response to strangers is the quickest test of how we are actually relating to God. Mindfulness is practical. Mindfulness is incarnational.

Some years ago, I was in Thailand visiting a Buddhist monastery. To get there, I had to rush for a train and fight for a seat. As I sat in it, hot and bothered, I suddenly noticed (after ten minutes or so) that there was a Buddhist monk sitting in front of me. I noticed him because he had not moved a muscle since I got on. My first thought was that he was dead; but, no, he was alive and probably more alive than the rest of us. Gradually, I felt his stillness communicate itself and influence the people in the crowded carriage around him. People did not look at him, speak to him, or discuss him. But his mindfulness was very much part of our group and a powerful influence on how we related to each other. The actively contemplative parts of our world, or our days, cannot always be justified in material terms; but without them, the quality of our lives are fatally impaired.

We in the West have much to learn from the East's reverence for mindfulness. Of course, it has a different connotation for us. For the Christian, mindfulness could be described as the experience of the presence of God or the practise of that presence. It is not thinking about God. To think about God all the day would make us distinctly odd and rather fanatical. We would end up riding roughshod over everyone who took our thoughts off God. But it is possible to practise the presence without mentally thinking of God.

Practising the presence is the meaning of meditation. It soon teaches us—socially and individually—how important it is that we meditate in order to become fearlessly and lovingly mindful. Mindfulness is the continuous lived knowledge that *being* underpins action. Being is the ground on which we act, the air in which we move. Everything we do is an expression of how and what we are. Meditation each day teaches us also that being is the powerful energy of regeneration, revitalisation, and healing. It resets the thermostat of our inner temperature and allows us to adjust the inner and outer levels with greater ease.

As the practise of meditation becomes the "whole of your life," as *The Cloud* says, you see how you can achieve more by slowing down but also when you need to speed up. The space in between the meditation periods then becomes connecting space, not a spiritual vacuum. In that space of each day, the fruits of the twice-daily meditation periods become evident. And one sees that the events of the day acquire meaning when they are seen as a preparation for the next meditation. Above all, you look forward to the next meditation as the return to the centre from which we all humanly, inevitably tend to drift. Many people tend to miss the evening meditation in their daily practise because the momentum of the day seems unstoppable or they are too tired. "I didn't get the chance to meditate today" should be inscribed as a warning over the lintels of homes and offices!

Yet the second meditation of the day teaches us how *being* can purify the whole day, re-centre us, and redeem the past by immersing it in the eternal now of God. To *be* is prayer. And to return to *being* in the midst of action transforms all we do into acts of prayer.

The first step to the recovery of mindfulness is perhaps not to meditate, but to see how much we have become unmindful. Until then, it will be difficult for us to see clearly enough what meditation really is and how important it is to embrace its work. Signs of mindlessness are not few, once we start seeing them. Socially, we see them in the patterns of behaviour around us that disturb and frighten us most: the uncontrollability of so many children; motorists shooting other motorists in "highway rage"; families and organisations acting dysfunctionally because people are too frightened to say the truth; structures of economic and social injustice that widen the gulf between the privileged and the marginalised; environmental pollution and ecological suicide made possible by short-term selfishness, lack of political ethics, obsession with profit, and the denial of death.

All of these symptoms of cultural un-mindfulness are exactly mirrored in us as individuals. Once we learn to see a few of the signs, we see too many for comfort. How quickly we can flare up in hostile anger, too easily justifying it by saying "it's better to express it." Anxiety that simmers in the silt of our souls even when we are having a good day. Hunger for sensational or expensive stimulation to replace our failing spirit of joy and delight in natural things. Rushing from one thing to another, complaining of too many things to do and not enough time to do them, and secretly addicted to it—a particular problem in monasteries. Scared to be alone. Forgetting the sense of the sacred in ordinary life. Lacking reverence in religious places and times of worship. Being indecisive, frightened to act, yet always impatient. Talking too much. Interrupting too often. Not listening to others.

The problem with mindless behaviour of this kind is that it cannot be stopped without becoming mindful. How can we recover mindfulness? How does a sleeping man wake up, or the unconsciousness become conscious? Most of our efforts to stop it are directed only at the symptoms of un-mindfulness rather than at its cause. And so, most remedies are not strong enough.

Jesus is a model of mindfulness, one who lived continuously in the presence of God. Perhaps his greatest act of mindfulness was his last when he forgave those who were killing him and understood that they could be forgiven because "they know not what they do." The mindful person is not only aware of the mindlessness of others, but is non-judgementally aware. A great peace awaits us when we realise that none of us has the right to speak or act as if we were superior to any other. The only authority most of us can claim or the saint *would* claim is the authority of failure rather than of success. Although we usually act on this awareness with a false humility when it suits us, we are quick, when offended, to condemn or criticise others with sweeping superiority. And then, words and comments that cannot easily be retracted are out of our mouths to upset the universe before we know what we have done.

Mindfulness *is* compassion. It limits the sway of evil in the world, and it can undo negative karma—as Jesus "took away the sins of the world" not by judging the world, but by loving it with the compassion of his mindfulness. It is possible to forgive human acts of evil when we perceive that they are produced by narrowness of outlook. Evil is not so much the wilful concentration of our energies on a deliberate wrong. It is rather the tragic foreshortening of consciousness to the key hole of the ego through we can only peep into reality. Through that narrow aperture, we see nothing but what affects our own pleasure or pain. Everything we see, we see from our isolated centre. We are mind-less, not mind-full. In that unmindful state, the world is illuminated by the dim, dreary light bulb of the ego rather than the daylight of God.

Once we have faced the uncomfortable symptoms of our unmindfulness, we must take up the practise of being mindful. The *idea* of mindfulness is not mindfulness. And the *wish* to be mindful that we all share is not the same as the work that realises it. Because mindfulness is essentially natural, life provides natural means both to recover it and to help it to grow. Ordinary life is made up of innumerable opportunities to be mindful which we carelessly squander.

When, for example, we take a break for a cup of tea and a biscuit, do we spend the time thinking of what we are going to do next (thereby eating too many biscuits) or to the simple enjoyment of the refreshment and the rest? Remembering this moment of thankfulness for food and drink, the sense of being nourished by the earth and human industry could make English tea drinkers the most mindful people on earth.

There are many other ways that daily life in our unmindful societies can re-centre us. Travelling is one of the most stressful of modern occupations, so we are told, as well as the biggest international industry. Yet the indignities of economy class can remind us humbly that the herd of humanity is not them but *us*. Enforced stretches of travel do not need to be filled with all the food and distractions on offer to anaesthetise us and prevent us from complaining. They can be used, as Bede Griffiths at the age of eight-five told me he enjoyed doing on planes, for solitude, reading, and meditation. Annoying delays or missed connections give us time to *be* rather than to fret and fume.

How many things in life do we say we "hate" doing? Housework, office work, accounts, or things we think demeaning or a waste of time. These are often the very opportunities to perform purifying rituals. The very triviality of the task makes it easier to see God through the performing of it mindfully, prayerfully. Every work can be begun and concluded with an act of mindfulness that, for the meditator especially, need not be a verbal act or even a thought. *The Cloud* speaks of meditation as a "naked stirring of love." Love does not require that we speak or think.

Every day has moments of enforced stillness or non-action: missing the bus, appointments coming late, going back to get something you forgot, looking high and low for something lost. These are often the occasions when we lose mindfulness: "fretting and fussing about so many things" as the unmindful Martha of the gospel is described doing, blaming others, sinking into despair, venting our anger on the guilty and the innocent alike. But the smallest stirring of consciousness can transform the moment of mindlessness into the practise of the presence of God.

The daily practise of meditation which roots the mantra deeply in the heart becomes an increasingly effective power of mindfulness throughout our lives. The mantra sounds in that depth of being where the mind of Christ fills us with its boundless experience of God and shares with us and all humanity the peace and joy of his spirit. As time passes, it becomes less necessary even to remember to say the mantra in times of mindlessness. By definition, it is difficult to remember what you have forgotten. But the Spirit, recalling what we have forgotten, employs the mantra as a sacrament of love and faith within us to come to our aid, to the constant assistance of our weakness.

Un-mindfulness separates us from that innate experience of the presence of God which sustains our sense of the sacred—in the stranger and the friend, at home and abroad. A false opposition then easily becomes established which sets the sacred against the secular, the material against the spiritual, the absolute against the relative. Because of this split in consciousness, we suffer from the guilt of feeling that we always fall short, and there is no lack of religious or other authorities to confirm our sense of sinfulness or inadequacy. Then, perhaps secretly, we rebel against being damned as sinners and rage at the god whose punishment we are taught to fear. Big splits start with small splinters. Once we have lost the unified vision of reality (of God) which mindfulness bestows, we are embarked on the steep descent into endless fragmentation: prejudice and endless conflict with those who differ from us in creed, colour, or culture.

Mindfulness could as well be called *heartfulness*. It is not an abstract, conceptual way of looking at the world. The mindful person is not an observer, an outsider, looking down or in or at. Certain techniques of mindfulness, helpful in themselves (like mindful walking, reading, eating, stopping for a moment at the chiming of the bell), can become separated from a more basic discipline of meditation and be seen as ends rather than means. They can then separate the person practising them from the "object" of their experience. The result of this would not be fully integrated human beings but spiritual eccentrics, what *The Cloud* calls false contemplatives, technicians rather than disciples.

The practise of the presence of God makes us fully human beings, not angelic entities. Mindfulness, for example, engenders hospitality, which is only truly hospitality when it is extended to strangers as well as friends, to the suspicious and the well-accredited. It engenders reverence for the sacred, not merely submission to the grand or the overpowering. It liberates humour, which allows us to live with paradox and to find joy in the depths of suffering. It keeps us humble, which allows us to treat everyone we meet as an equal and so avoid the twin dangers of negative and positive projection. We are humbly, humanly able to live with failure without the self-indulgence of guilt or perfectionism. We are able to look into the eyes of our ego, our mirror-mind, without fear, without self-infatuation and to love it into submission to the true Self. Mindfulness is the poise of being human.

We encounter the fully mindful human being in the Jesus of the gospel. We should only remember that if we do meet the real Jesus in the gospels, it is because the mind of the risen Jesus is in us as we read or hear the stories of his life.

One like us in all things except wilful distraction, Jesus lived in a continuous and constantly growing practise of the presence of God. St John portrays this most powerfully by emphasising the complete other-centredness of Jesus in the consciousness of the *Father*. "He who sent me is present with me and has not left me alone . . . in all I say I have been taught by my Father" (Jn 8:27). "I have set before you many good deeds, done by my Father's power" (Jn 10:32). "Know that the Father is in me, and I in the Father" (Jn 10:38). Yet, this other-centredness explains both the unshakeable rootedness of Jesus in his true Self and the authority of his personality and teaching. He was always aware of his Father even in the final desolation and abandonment of his death: "My God, my God, why have you abandoned me!" (Mt 27:46). And later, "into your hands I commend my spirit."

It was into his Father's hands that Jesus could commend his departing spirit because he had lived to the full the mindfulness of his own Kingdom message: that the Kingdom or presence of God is within us. Whatever happens to us, we cannot be separated from this presence. In each story of the gospel, we encounter the mind of Christ and his mindfulness—his practise of the presence of God which began, developed naturally, and has reached its completion in the Spirit.

Let's end this letter with one of those stories. Jesus is on his way to the house of Jairus whose daughter had just died:

> And while Jesus was on his way he could hardly breathe for the crowds. Among them was a woman who had suffered from haemorrhages for twelve years; and nobody had been able to cure her. She came up from behind and touched the edge of his cloak, and at once her haemorrhage stopped. Jesus said, "Who was it that touched me?" All disclaimed it, and Peter and his companions said, "Master, the crowds are hemming you in and pressing upon you." But Jesus said, "Someone did touch me, for I felt that power had gone out from me." Then the woman, seeing that she was detected, came trembling and fell at his feet. Before all the people she explained why she had touched him and how she had been instantly cured. He said to her, "My daughter, your faith has cured you. Go in peace." (Lk 8:43–48, New English Bible)

This moving story, which seems to tell us both of an incident in the life of Jesus and the experience of Christ in the early church, is full of mindfulness and its fruits. First, there is the self-recollection of Jesus in the turmoil of the pressing crowd. He remains centred in his own solitude and does not have his identity scattered in the images that people have of him. This allows him to relate to the crowd as a group of people with individual needs and personalities, not as a crowd of followers or supporters. Feeling himself touched, he asks *who* had touched him and persists in asking until the woman comes forward.

At first, his exposing her might seem harsh: dragging her into publicity, ashamed as she is of her embarrassing illness, ritually impure, excluded from others, and guilty of making Jesus similarly impure by touching him (even just as a woman). Yet, she then does the unexpected: she announces what she had kept secret. In her doing this, the real miracle of the story is revealed because her twelve years of isolation and shame are ended—she is restored not only to health but self-worth. The mindfulness of Jesus is evident not only in his feeling a special touch in the crowd, but in his compassionate completion of the cure as he gently pushes her back into human dignity. Finally, he reminds her it was not his magic but her faith, her capacity for relationship with him, which has made her whole again in every sense.

The edge of Jesus' Jewish garments had ritual tassels. It was these the woman touched in her desperation and with her faith. Today it is the interior mindfulness of Christ we brush against in our need and brokenness, our distraction and daily un-mindfulness.

We are not expected to be pure before we touch him, whatever the pharisee of our guilty ego, or other types of pharisee, may say. All we need is sufficient awareness to recognise the greater mind that dwells in us and to trust that that mind is full of the compassionate heart of God. In meditation, we begin to *touch* that mind and gradually to be drawn deeper and deeper into oneness with it and so with what it is one with. Little by little, our mindfulness becomes his.

Let us keep each other in mind and heart, grateful for the Way we share.

With much love

Laurence

Laurence Freeman, OSB

Letter Four

21 September 1996
Feast of St Matthew

Clarity

Dearest friends,

The Benedictine monastery of San Miniato stands on a hill contemplating the city of Florence, and the city of Florence looks up and contemplates San Miniato. This mutual gaze has endured nearly a thousand years. To stand in the piazza in front of the monastery looking down on the red-roofed city and the great maternal dome of the cathedral is to feel why a place of worship has stood here long before temple gave way to church and why worshippers, pilgrims, meditators, tourists, and courting couples all still feel deeply at home in its benevolent and hospitable presence.

During my stay at San Miniato after the John Main Seminar to prepare for the beginning of a meditation centre at the monastery, we celebrated the feast of the birth of the Blessed Virgin and the seven hundredth anniversary of the founding of the cathedral. That evening, the great dome by Brunelleschi, the tower by Giotto, and the Baptistery were bedecked with burning torches that kept their vigil until the early hours of the following morning. The weather had been variable, cloudy and rainy; but on this morning, the air was brilliantly, virginally clear. Looking down on the city on my way to morning prayer, I could pick out, with a new acuity, details of the buildings and see with feeling the texture of the river at which I had been looking for a week. The view had seemed magnificent and new each time I had looked at it. But, by contrast with this sharp, fresh clarity, I felt I had never seen it until that moment.

Clarity is a beautiful word in English. The dictionary gives it six-teen meanings. It can be used as a verb, as in *to clear a path*; as an adjective, as in *clear weather* or a *clear complexion*; and as a noun, as *to be in the clear*. Language reflects reality here because clarity is an experience of wholeness and of the integration of the different parts of our being. We are clear, we clarify, and we are in clarity simulta-neously. To be a clear person is to contribute to the clarification of the world in which you live.

Clarity is a natural virtue. Everyone agrees that it is better to be clear than obscure even if they differ about what clarity may be. A clearly expressed idea, a clear theatrical or musical performance, a poignant-ly expressed image in a poem, an elegant mathematical equation are applauded because they communicate the delight and freshness which are associated with the dispelling of confusion or darkness. Forces of darkness that overlay clarity with confusion or deception— a lie, an act of vandalism or terrorism, exploitative relationships—are unacceptable even when their perpetrators claim a rationale for what they are doing. We love clarity because it enables us to love better.

Seeing the beauty of a clear morning over Florence when the wind and the prayer of thanksgiving have swept away the pollution that obscures the view is a natural delight. The eye sees, and the mind enjoys. Clarity of the senses is an eloquent metaphor, even a sacrament, of the mental clarity which allows consciousness to expand. All consciousness is evolving. It has evolved in creation from mineral to vegetable, and it continues to grow at the human level. Why should we think that the level of consciousness with which we are now gifted is the highest of which we are capable? The earliest Christian thinkers asserted confidently that the desti-nation of human consciousness was nothing less than divinisation, to see and know all from the one universal centre, sharing in the divine life by grace. Religious leaders and teachers since have not always been so strong in reminding people of this exhortation to share in the clarity of God. As historical institutions, religions develop vested interests in power structures that seem easier to maintain when people are encouraged to underestimate their potential. But the hunger for clarity, which is a manifestation of the human aspiration for God, is irrepressible. What we call the spiritual hunger or the hunger for prayer today is simply a reassertion of this aspiration which no human power structure can extinguish.

Clarity is the nature of things. It is the nature of consciousness itself. So, to make something clear, we do not have to add anything but simply, and usually with difficulty, to remove whatever obscures or pollutes its essential nature. This applies as much to the planetary environment as to human consciousness. Seeing how this applies across the board of reality helps to illuminate the intertwining of our three eyes of perception. The physical eye and the senses can be handicapped or damaged, and they can often be improved, sometimes healed. But as soon as some degree of sensory perception is acknowledged, the eye of the mind is activated. We assess what we are perceiving and try to give it meaning. If something happens to us that seems meaningless, if we cannot "see what it means," we feel deeply uneasy and go in search of an explanation. When one level of perception is not sound, it is likely that the other levels will also suffer. How else could we see the pollution and destruction of the green spaces on which we depend for physical and psychological well-being and not understand clearly what we are doing? When the senses and the mind have lost their clarity and harmony, as has happened in our culture of exploitation and the cult of progress, a deep healing from another source is required.

Our hope for salvation is the third eye. Restoring health to the eye of the heart, as St Augustine said, is the work of meditation and love. It is the purity of heart which Jesus said is the condition of seeing God in all things. Although clarity is entirely natural, it demands work. One of the dictionary definitions for *clear* is to be unencumbered. When we clear our desks or clear up an untidy room, we experience at one level what we are doing at another level in meditation. It brings with it a sense of satisfaction, a lightness of being, and the relief of returning chaos to good order. St Benedict taught that in the monastery all things should be done in good order so that no one in the house should be disturbed. Every good parent knows how important it is to create a well-ordered, punctual, clean home where children can learn and grow peacefully, however difficult it may be today to achieve that.

Buddhists speak of the afflicted states of mind from which every person suffers and which we must all learn how to transform. These are the clouding, polluting forces of fear, anger, resentment, pride, and desire which can sweep over us like seasonal storms and leave us battered and repentant. Every contemplative tradition recognises and warns its practitioners about the purgative way, the clearing and cleansing of our inner rooms. This insight is at the heart of the Christian idea of sin and penance. John Cassian, like all true teachers, was less concerned with moralising, condemnation, or punishment when he thought about sin than with its effective uprooting. He explained how we must:

> unload all our vices and rid our souls of the wreck and rubble of passion. Then simplicity and humility must be laid as sure foundations on the living solid earth of our hearts. If we wish our prayer to reach upward to the heavens and beyond we must ensure that our mind is cleared of every earthly defect and cleansed of passion's grip and is so light of itself that its prayer, free of sin's weighty load, will rise upward to God. (*Conf.* 9:2, 4)

On the "solid earth of our hearts," the tower of holiness arises. But as the psalm says, the builders of great towers labour in vain if the Lord does not work with them. The work of clarification is co-operative. We are spiritual entrepreneurs at our peril. This is a peculiar danger of our own time when we place so much emphasis on our own resources and look upon outside help as something we can buy or control. It is not easy to be mature disciples today, even of the Spirit. The mantra teaches us how to approach this delicate dilemma by the degree of effort it demands at the beginning and the serious commitment it involves day after day. But as the mantra becomes rooted in our consciousness, opening within us the clear stream of the prayer of the Spirit, less effort is required. The mantra is always a sacrament of faith. And the discipline remains constant. However long you have been meditating, you will be inclined on certain occasions to go for a walk or watch the evening news rather than to do your practise.

So much attention has been given to the idea of surrender in our spirituality that we can forget the egotistical flavour of *my* choosing to surrender to God. It can be a helpful ideal to launch a spiritual

path; but as one gets into it, it becomes obvious that we have to surrender the very idea of surrender. Relaxing the will is perhaps a better way to express what the call to surrender is saying. Learning this
in meditation makes it easier to practise it also in our relationships.
Rather than trying to love others so hard that we end up hating
them for making us feel like failures, we learn totally to relax the
will to love and find that loving becomes a great deal easier. This
approach to the surrender of the ego to God also allows the natural fruits of meditation to manifest in a way that we can enjoy
because we are not seeking them. The best gifts are unsought.

A woman once went to a spiritual teacher to ask for advice on
how she could become enlightened. He told her to live austerely,
with complete self-control, in solitude in a mountain cave, and to
meditate twenty hours a day. This she did. After twenty years and
no enlightenment, she walked back to the teacher struggling with
her terrible disappointment. He listened attentively and then half-
apologised for her fruitless labours. "But maybe you are just not
meant to be enlightened. So go back and just get on with your life."
As she did not have many career opportunities by this stage, she
returned to her cave and got on with daily life. She sat to meditate
as usual but with one great difference. She no longer had any
expectation or desire to be enlightened. She was instantly enlightened. As she walked back down the mountain to see the teacher,
she thought she heard his gentle laughter in the wind around her.

Clarity is transparent. On a beautiful clear day, the light in
which we see everything seems to radiate out from within everything we are looking at. On a face with a beautiful complexion, the
light of inner health and well-being seems to shine on the skin, as
it did in the Transfiguration of Jesus. The work of becoming clear
is not enhanced by ego-driven austerity programmes that we
employ as tools, like a burglar trying to break into the house of
God. All this can be even worse than counter-productive. It is the
ego itself that has to be gently but firmly eased away, like a pro-
tective film that is peeled off a lens to allow greater translucency.
Otherwise, we can be like people trying to clean a dirty wind-
screen with a dirty cloth.

Buddhists speak of the "clear light of emptiness." It is a beautiful
phrase on which readers of the gospels can reflect. It helps us to

understand the Christian insight that God is light without any shadow. This light is incarnated in Jesus, the light of the world, which shines like a steady flame in a place without wind, which is at the still centre of the human nature in each person. The darkness in which it shines does not affect it, even though it will overwhelm us who still live in the shadows of death. But the steadiness of the light is our hope that we are journeying with a purpose into pure light. The emptiness of God is as necessary to understand. The very event of the Incarnation was, as we are told in the New Testament, a divine self-emptying. If there were no divine emptiness, the infinite fullness of God would not be able to fill it.

Poverty of spirit is our emptiness being transformed in the clear light of God's empty fullness. Unless we can become poor in spirit, we cannot divest ourselves of the many layered films of obscuring thoughts and feelings which block the light from passing into and through us. As we become poor, we must learn not to settle for any lesser clarity than the total clarity for which we are destined. Because emptiness is so wonderful an experience, such an unloading of unnecessary anxiety and egotism, we can easily become possessive of the peace it bestows. This would then subtly put the ego back in control; and if it is responsible for its own dethroning, we will have to wait a long time. Out of this "grand poverty" as Cassian describes it, penetrating insights can arise into ourselves and the nature of the world or of God. Someone I met once liked to take a pencil and notebook into their meditation room to record these insights for posterity! At the time of the work, no gift should be sought or be turned into a possession. We will learn much more, much more quickly, if we are content to come out of the meditation knowing less than we thought we knew before. We will not have more knowledge but greater clarity. And the clarity we are speaking about is the highest form of knowledge.

"I have not gone after things too great for me," the psalm says. Clarity allows small things to shine with significance. In a culture that worships size and power, this will be a valuable lesson. St Benedict also knew that what he called the "divinising light" is best transmitted through an appreciation and reverence for the ordinary rather than by an attempt to create the extraordinary. When we see clearly, we see what we have always seen, but we see it each time with the freshness and virginal wonder of the first time. Small things teach us most. The best spiritual teachers, for example, use the fewest words. But they teach by their smallest gestures and daily habits. To see a peaceful and centred person answer a phone, cope with a traffic jam, or deal with a domestic crisis is to learn more in experience about the spiritual reality than the best talks or the most difficult books could ever give. In the gospel stories, we encounter to some degree the Jesus who impressed his contemporaries as much by his presence and integrated being as by his words. The silence of action is stronger than words.

If you are walking in the street and see a flower, you smell it, mentally name it, *rose* or *dahlia*, and walk on. But to name it can be to demean its uniqueness, and the label can obscure the light it emits. In its unrepeatable uniqueness, the flower has no name except itself—the secret name known only to God, who is its being. The light of being is the uniqueness of everything, and it is also its manifestation of God who delights in the liberty of each particle of the cosmos. Clarity of consciousness changes the way we see the world ("a new creation") because it both reveals and affirms the uniqueness of all things.

If we can learn to see and reverence this in small things, we will be able to do the same with every person we meet. Then even without our knowing it, we will be loving God. It is impossible to treat others cruelly or with prejudice if we have clearly seen their uniqueness. It is only when the labels obscure the light—Serb or Muslim, Jew or Arab, Catholic or Protestant, black or white—that human beings can be capable of their characteristic inhumanity to one another and even to justify it by the labels that incite their rage. Clear awareness of our anger and other passions is the best means of preventing the retaliation or escalation of volume which happens whenever anger is self-indulgently expressed. Clarity is all-forgiving. When we see clearly, there is no place for guilt or self-rejection because these are more often than not the cause of much of our obscurity.

The church is commissioned to forgive, not to condemn. In the clarity of Christ, it should be the human institution which most strongly opposes the rule of violence, intolerance, and the depersonalisation of society and culture. Of all organisations, it should most courageously show how we can clearly live by seeing the divine light in each other. But because the church is a human organisation, it easily falls into the general pattern of judging and labeling that obscures the true nature of people. However, in the radical change which is taking place around it, the church is seeing its organisation crumbling in a way that is as shocking to many Christians as the fall of the temple, which Jesus prophesied, must have been to its regular worshippers. When any great house collapses, you see something gleaming in the rubble which was its most precious object. Today, the church is learning to see itself as more than a religious institution. With clarity, it can learn again to see itself as the body of Christ which like every living thing is growing and changing and which like all bodies can at times be sick. We know that its full growth will be co-extensive with the universe; and in its mystical reality, no labels apply: neither Greek nor Jew, male nor female. Churchmen are often quick to say that we are still struggling here on earth, bills have to be paid and offices have to be maintained and that this full realisation is yet to happen and should not be anticipated because the boat should not be rocked any further.

In a sense, they are right but their sobriety must be complemented by the intoxication of the spiritual teachers of Christianity. Through history, the great contemplatives have built up a tradition which is now reaching maturity. As individuals, they experienced something which as a community we are all today being asked to discover as a universal invitation and potential. They were not as eccentric as they seemed at the time nor so unorthodox as they were often treated. They were the prophets of what the church essentially is and the forerunners of what the church is to be.

Clarity happens when the mind is calm. Our meditation is the daily work of calming the mind and allowing the Spirit to employ our consciousness, at those times of silence, in collaboration with its grace for our healing and growth. We all know our attention flickers. The slightest wind can ruffle the surface of the calmest water. But the surface is not what we are concerned with. The depth of being, deeper than we can penetrate with our curious, observing minds, is where we find the sharpest clarity. Our afflicted states, our passions, and our sinfulness do not penetrate to this depth or affect the purity of our identity as divine icons. Coming to this depth is the work of the whole of each day. If meditation were only a matter of two periods a day, it would be no more than a technique for temporarily calming the surface. In fact, the work of meditation goes on continuously, and the regular periods are significant for reminding us that every moment is prayer.

Clarity is always surprising. It allows us to see everything within the present moment which is a constantly deepening entry into the eternal now of God. But it is also wonderfully reassuring because when we see clearly we recognise everything with a friendly feeling of familiarity. This is because we are seeing in the light of the true self, where all divisions, including the most basic division between *me* and the *world*, are dissolved. Meditators of all traditions discover this perception of community and friendship with each other even when they do not know each other's name or even speak their language. It is all the more odd then that we should fear clarity as much as we do.

A little clarity is always welcome, but too much threatens our defence systems and our sense of security. This is why spiritual progress is so often a pattern of recurrent near misses. We frequently trip ourselves up and lose patience or the courage to be still for that extra moment. Distractions and anxieties become easy excuses for slipping back into the shadows because the light is too bright, too glorious. Ezekiel saw the glory of God and of the Son of Man in an overwhelming vision in which everything was burning with light. A fourteenth-century English translation of a familiar verse from St John's Gospel illustrates that the true nature of clarity is the glory of God and the glory of God is when we become fully alive.

> I have clarified thee on earth by completing the work which thou gavest me to do; and now Father, clarify me in thy own presence with the clarity which I had with thee before the world began. (Jn 17:4)

One of the tests of authentic beauty is that it makes people happy. So does clarity. The beauty of God, God's glory, is the divine clarity, the light of love. And the sign of that love is in the capacity we each possess for total clarity of consciousness. In the thrilling words of St Basil, "the human being is an animal who has received the vocation to become God." Experience shows us that when we are clear, we are in touch with our goodness as a participation in the divine Good. We see the goodness at the core of ourselves; and, therefore, we speak, act, feel, and think more lovingly and more consistently. Meditation is a simple path that removes the daily obscurities that make us forget or doubt our essential clarity. And it is more, because it takes us each day a little deeper into the light which has no shadow.

With much love

Laurence

Laurence Freeman, OSB

Letter Five

30 December 1996
Anniversary of John Main

The Punctuality of the Spirit

Dearest friends,

In October and November, I made a long trip to North and South America. My principal work was the usual: the very enriching work, for me, of giving retreats and talks on meditation and of meditating and being with some of the individuals and groups who form our silent "monastery without walls" around the world. But I had also accepted the suggestion of the American publisher of *The Good Heart* to do what I could to help promote the book. Before long, a full schedule of talks in bookstores and media interviews had been arranged to fit in with the retreats I was to be giving.

But perhaps we learn more from what (we think) we do badly than from what we assume we do well. Standing up in the middle of strange bookstores and speaking to a distracted handful of passing customers and the few others who had seen the advertising is good for anyone's humility. I was later to learn that the commercial advantage of such events is not thought to be the speaker's presentation on the evening, but all the associated advance publicity. These launches, then, were often non-events, impossible to evaluate, needing to be done, involving great poverty of spirit, and very helpful in shattering illusions about oneself. Just like meditation.

We are all quick to form habits. Perhaps they serve as walls against the ocean of chaos that we fear surrounds us. After the first couple of launches, I had begun to develop a pattern which worked for all those which followed: a talk on the background of the book and of the work of the community, readings from the book, a description of the seminar with the Dalai Lama and of how important meditation had been to the spirit of dialogue. Then a short period of meditation followed, which I was both surprised and pleased to see everyone who had come was happy with. In some stores, we must have made a weird sight, twenty or so people sitting meditating among the bookshelves as customers wandered around, coffee machines fizzed, and cash registers tinkled. After the meditation, we enjoyed for a few moments that feeling of peace and trust which people who have meditated together find themselves to have received, though they do not know how. This was the pattern of the bookstore launches. Obviously, it was a pattern I had drawn from the meditation group, the simplest of all patterns for a spiritual meeting: teaching, silence, sharing.

After a dozen or so such events, I was less bothered by the commercial setting and came to see these events as a form of spiritual meeting. Even though for the bookstore staff (who often joined us for the meditation), the PR organiser, and the publisher it may have had other meanings and another purpose, it was also a small ephemeral meditation group. This dawned on me when I noticed how seriously people were listening to the words of Jesus which I read as part of the extract from the Dalai Lama's commentary on the gospels. I realised how rarely one sees people listening to the words of the gospel with such eager and hungry attention.

In a similar way, we can discover how all of the trivial or routine or irksome activities of daily life have an invisible spiritual significance. Nothing is without meaning if it is done with reverence— "for the glory of God" as St Paul says. The catalyst which can make that invisible dimension suddenly perceptible and deeply moving is the Word of God. In the Letter to the Colossians, Paul says that Christ is the visible image of the invisible God, the Word which communicates the silent hidden thought and makes it sound and resonate in the minds and hearts of others. As I sensed the gospel's power to manifest this living Word of spiritual awareness, I began to think about the significance of this event for Christian faith today. Curious, I thought, that people were listening to the words of Jesus so eagerly and openly here in bookstores surrounded by special offers and the mass marketing of the consumer society.

Curious that, amid so many other words, the Word could rise above them with such a clear articulation, like a single beautiful voice above the roar of a crowd.

If I was in fact preaching the gospel in the marketplace without having realised at first that I was doing so, it was in a new context. I was not trying to sell Christian faith as a better product than any other faith. I was not trying to sell it at all. Maybe not being a good salesperson is a prerequisite for a modern missionary. Yet, while speaking about a book on inter-religious dialogue, I was helping people to make their own contact with the gospel, just by reading the words of Jesus. The meaning of that contact for them would unfold in their own special circumstances which might or might not be one that official Christianity recognised or approved. Perhaps one of the perplexing dilemmas for traditional Christianity today is the meaning of communicating the gospel in a non-competitive way in the context of relationships with other faiths.

For the exclusivist Christian, this is nonsensical. And yet, it is what is happening all around us all the time today. And perhaps through this new articulation of the Word Made Flesh in relation to the other faiths by which people experience God, the Spirit is trying to teach us something. Perhaps Christianity is learning that if it is truly universal, it must find and recognise itself in all forms of human spiritual experience and in every kind of spiritual event.

> His approach is gentle, his presence fragrant, his yoke very light; rays of light and knowledge shine forth before him as he comes. He comes with the heart of a true protector; he comes to save, to heal, to teach, to admonish, to strengthen, to console, to enlighten the mind, first of the person who receives him, then through that person the minds of others also. The person deemed worthy of the Holy Spirit is enlightened in soul and sees beyond the power of human sight what he did not know before. (St Cyril of Jerusalem, *Instructions to Catechumens*)

To be open to the Spirit who opens our eyes and to see the risen Christ is to know that we are always being taught something new about the meaning and wonder of Jesus.

One of the early Fathers said that "there is no such thing as delay with the Holy Spirit." This means that everything happens at the right moment. We often say that as a pious platitude when there seems nothing else to say. We say it to others in distress although we cannot believe it when we are in distress ourselves. But when we reflect upon the pattern of our lives, the ever-changing pattern, it is difficult not to feel that there is a story unfolding; and that deep inside the story there is guiding and protecting power. If this is not a false consolation or self-deception, then it is a truth which illuminates each person's life and the story of creation and also the history of the church. The fact (whether we feel enthusiastic or threatened by it) that we have entered an era of inter-religious dialogue is a timely fact. If it is not random, it must be guided. This is the kairos moment of Christianity now. And if to be a Christian always involves the privilege and duty of communicating Christ to the world, then we must find a way to do so which is true to the present kairos.

At Christmas, we reflect on the birth of Jesus as the incarnation of the eternal word "in the fullness of time." He was punctual. And if Jesus arrived right on time, so our response to that temporal and timeless event must be always contemporary, up to the moment. At the end of his life when he faced his human appointment with death, Jesus also recognised that his time had come (Jn 17:1). The time we are dealing with in this spiritual recognition is not merely chronological. There are no clocks in heaven. It is time in the sense of how things in flux are related to each other and all together to their common source, the universal reference point of God.

Some things make the time right simply by happening when they do, although it may take us a lifetime to accept what has happened, to see it as part of the meaningful pattern of our life. This is particularly true for things that happen that cause us pain or bewilder us because they take us so much by surprise. The Spirit has not deserted us even when we feel that life is a desert of inexplicable suffering or of meaningless routine as so many people do today. Indeed, it is in this very human struggle to awaken to God that the Spirit is most humanly and most intimately present to us in the Mind of Christ. Teaching, healing, strengthening, consoling, enlightening us all by stages according to the natural laws of our personal growth. And teaching us that the quickest way to arrive is to be patient.

The timeliness of events is no less true when it applies to the history of religion. We are today arriving in a new era of religious dialogue, of tolerance, of mutual reverence, and of learning from each other which our forebears could never have imagined. Yet, its rightness for Christians is attested by the fact that it is so compatible with the personality and example of Jesus. He rejected no one, tolerated all, and saw the mystery of God in all people and in nature. He ate with those he should have despised, he spoke with those he should have avoided. He was as open to others as he was to God. And so, to accept the punctuality of the Spirit in opening Christian faith to this era of inter-religious dialogue helps Christians to know and love Jesus more fully: Jesus in whom the inexhaustible mysteries of God are contained.

At Christmas and at all other anniversaries of birth and death, we remember. This is not merely nostalgia, living regretfully in the past, discontented with the present, or unhappy about how things are now. To remember truly is to live more fully in the present, and the act of remembering is the heart of all religious ritual. In the mass, we remember the Last Supper as well as every other celebration of the Eucharist from Calvary to the present day. To remember is literally "to call to mind." It is, therefore, to be reminded of that from which our distractedness and forgetfulness frequently disconnect us. When you go online on the Internet, it is with the help of a modem attached to your computer that connects your phone line to the great mind of the World Wide Web. The technology and the very concept of this world wide network of (almost) instantaneous communication is fantastic. But it is also very fallible precisely because it is only technology. In the middle of an E-mail message or some other transaction, the connection can suddenly and inexplicably be lost, and a little message might appear on your screen to ask if you would like to be reconnected.

The Holy Spirit in a similar way intervenes punctually at the exact moment of need in the midst of our human fallibility. She does not demand anything, only asking if we want to be reconnected. Sometimes the screen message, it is true, asks if you want more information; if you are curious as to why you became disconnected, you can click on "yes" but most of the time you are more eager to start again than to analyse what went wrong. (Mistakes like sins happen after all, and we do not have to understand the technology of everything.)

To be re-remembered, re-connected, is an act of redemption, of ever-available compassion which over a lifetime becomes an embedded pattern. We get into the habit of living consciously, of seeing God in all things from bookstores to churches. We learn to believe that we are loved. Good habits drive out bad ones. And we can only interpret one kind of pattern with the help of another. By remembering, we are not just thinking about the past. We are developing insight into the pattern of past, present, and future. We practise repentance in doing this because we quickly see how often our past mistakes arose from our living in the past or the future; we become trapped in past patterns that lose their capacity to change and develop into new ones, or adrift in the future in swirls of impatience, anxiety, or fantasy.

The making flesh of the eternal Word happened at a historical moment, but it also happens in every moment. To be conscious of this incarnation is contemplation, and to remain conscious of it requires the work of meditation. In meditation, we allow patterns to re-form and to be reformed, old patterns to dissolve, and new, freer, and more spontaneous ones to develop in our minds and hearts. Without this continuous work of prayer, of being re-membered to reality, we too often miss the gift of the moment because we are thinking of what we have lost or what we are hoping will happen tomorrow. This is why meditation is about living in the moment of Christ as John Main understood so deeply. It is not about thinking of Christ as he was or how he will come again but about being with him now and being transformed in his being. This is not a static historical moment but a flowing, a flowering, and an unfolding of the mystery of being itself. To look lovingly at the baby Jesus in the crib is not a sentimental act, therefore, but a profound reflection on the mystery of being. The prologue to the Gospel of John ("In the beginning was the Word . . .") shows how early Christians realised that in Jesus the deepest mysteries of the universe could be understood in the mind of God.

In Jesus, time and eternity intersect, the Word becomes human words. But the intersection happens in human poverty of spirit. Poverty is the point "where infinite mystery meets concrete existence." Poverty is not only the absence of things but the awareness of our need for others, for God. Human neediness is universal. The richest and the most powerful, like the poorest and most marginalised, are all equally in need. Need is simply the strong feeling that arises in response to the fact of interdependence. We are not separate from each other or from God. Wisdom is the recognition of our inter-relatedness. Compassion is the practise of our connectedness. In meditation, we dive to a level of reality deeper than that of our surface, ego-driven minds which so often are caught in the net of the illusion of our independence and isolation. Untangling from that net is the daily work of meditation, and it is also the new pattern of the practise of the presence of God in ordinary life which is created by daily meditation.

Meditation helps us to embrace the wonder of our poverty, our need for God. It is the first level of true happiness according to the Beatitudes: Happy are the poor in spirit (those who know their need for God) for theirs is the kingdom of heaven. Our worldly minds reject that as nonsense even though they may pay pious lip-service to it. We are happy, the ego says, because we have met our needs and protected ourselves from the vulnerability which human need exposes. The word teaches us something different, which we are reluctant to learn. The remembering we do at Christmas and other anniversaries of birth and death makes us more teachable. Like Mary, we learn to ponder the mysteries of being made visible in Jesus and to wait a lifetime for the pondering to have its full effect.

The ordinariness of the circumstances of Jesus' birth, his low socioeconomic and cultural position in the world, are not, therefore, mere historical accidents. Or they are accidents with a message. It is somehow more appropriate that the Word should become flesh in the manger of human poverty than in the palaces of power and privilege. He is closer to the universal human condition of need, of inter-relatedness. An inevitable consequence of this is to tip the scales of power back to balance by restoring the dignity of significance to the poor, the homeless, the bereaved, the voiceless. It is more than a coincidence that not only Jesus but every great spiritual teacher has especially loved the poor, because to see their spiritual significance beneath the appearance of social uselessness and the embarrassment they make the affluent feel is to celebrate a sacrament of God. To truly see them is to truly see God. Wherever human beings recognise and accept their own and others' poverty, they recognise and accept Christ.

Seeing is believing. Only if we see God can we really believe in God. But there are degrees of seeing, and it takes time to get our vision clear and sharp. Time is the school of enlightenment for us, individually, in our brief lives, just as it is for the story of creation in which we find our meaning, as well as for the manifestation of the true meaning and purpose of the church in the history of salvation.

Today as we try so hard to speed up the processes of nature, to reduce the time it takes to do anything, it is difficult to trust that the Spirit does not delay. Conservatives try to put the clock back thinking that something has gone wrong or because they are too threatened by change to trust the power of God to sort things out. Radicals become angrily impatient and try to effect change without passing through the stages of growth which all living things must obey. Are we travelling too fast or not fast enough? It is of course all a matter of perspective.

While I was on my long trip, I was frequently getting on planes to be hurled around the earth at five hundred miles an hour. I often used the opportunity to prepare my talks on stillness. And to meditate at my regular times. The speed of modern life is external. Even the psychological acceleration of experience that causes so much stress and anxiety for people today is—relative to the depths of the mind of Christ in us and to our own spirit—superficial. However fast we are moving, we can pause to find the still point of the Spirit. We just need to be reminded of its existence more frequently today. Travelling by plane or car gives an illusion of physical stillness. We are moving fast, but we can do things, like eat and drink and read, that we can only do when we are still. At this level, it is all maya, illusion, relative reality.

Even in the midst of daily illusion, we can stop and plunge into the reality in which we move and live and know our being. In meditation, we learn to relate the speed of outer life to the stillness of the spirit, which is the speed of now. We learn to relate the inner emptiness of poverty of spirit to the overflowing fullness of multiple plans, desires, and dreams. Once the discipline of meditation has started to become a liberating pattern in our lives, we become aware how important it is to relate the inner and the outer, the absolutely real and the relatively real. We sense that we cannot properly perform our external activities unless we are at least partially familiar with the stillness, the emptiness within ourselves. If we run from inner emptiness into external fullness, we will find only the anguish of hollowness. To ignore or deny the pure unbounded openness of the spirit in our inner poverty is to make ourselves dangerously vulnerable to our inner demons and illusions.

Without the strength of the spiritual reality, these dark shadows of the psyche control us from the unconscious. Our deeply engrained patterns of fear, self-rejection, and desire send out signals that confuse the imagination, disrupt our hold on reality, and produce destructive and self-destructive behaviour. What we see in the psychopaths and sociopaths on the news each day is present in each of us to a lesser degree.

It is not necessary to sit dead still for hours in front of a brick wall to be enlightened. The Incarnation teaches us that it is only necessary to be healthy. To be balanced. To be fully and ordinarily human. That is one reason why it is so important to be reminded that we are not looking for anything out of the ordinary when we meditate. What seems extraordinary today will seem very ordinary tomorrow if the natural stages of growth are allowed to occur in the guided sequence of the Spirit's punctuality. Martha will slow down and take time to meditate and learn not to be anxious when important guests arrive. Mary will get up from meditation and set the table at the right time. The only additional element in our lives that most of us need is a discipline of regular, short periods of meditation. That is the little bit of leaven that will help the dough of our lives to rise.

To allow that pattern of daily meditation to take hold amid all the other patterns of our lives, not just imaginatively but actually, is a challenge for the best of us and to the best in us. It is a mundane introduction to the cosmic law of sacrifice. There is an Indian story which tells how Vishnu came every day to offer worship to Shiva by offering a thousand lotuses at her feet. One day, after a few thousand years of such worship, he discovered as he lay the lotuses down that there were only 999 that day. (Such things happen occasionally.) Without delay, he plucked out one of his eyes, beautiful and shaped like a lotus, and completed the offering with it by placing it among the 999.

Worship is another way of understanding the self-renunciation which is the dynamic at the heart of meditation and of all love. It offers us a different way of looking at sacrifice: not as a loss of something precious, something dragged from us as we kick and scream interiorly, but as a precious opportunity to enter even greater bliss and fulfilment. To accept and to give in such moments is a gift of praise which collects our whole being and unifies and simplifies us in the sudden alchemy of love.

This is the multi-dimensional work of the mantra in meditation, and it is why we must be so simple in our saying of the mantra if all these dimensions are to be harmonised and develop together. It is not only a sacrifice of time—we must be the first culture on earth to think that prayer is essentially a spare-time activity. The sacrifice includes our thoughts and imagination, the hundred-and-one conversations at all levels of our mind. As it was for Vishnu, it is an offering of our whole way of seeing and knowing, a temporary, partial blindness which is an act of faith in another and greater way of seeing and knowing.

The mantra introduces us into an experience of prayer, a spontaneous act of praise, which involves our whole being, and not just telling God with our linguistic minds how omnipotent, omniscient, and omnipresent "he" is, but accepting the invitation inherent in our very existence to become as God is: by grace, by adoption, by love. In this co-operation of grace and nature, our being is made whole. Christ the healer is most at work uniting depth and surface, inner and outer, in the pure gift of praise which is ours and his as we listen to the mantra. As Fr John taught, our meditation becomes most purely prayer not just in the work of saying the mantra in the face of distraction but in the ease of listening to it.

Meditation is, therefore, both sacrifice and praise: the sacrifice of praise. To practise meditation is the only way to learn what meditation means and how its meaning is much more than it may seem to those who want to get something short-term out of it; and much, much more than those who think that by meditating they are making something happen. By learning to meditate, we come to understand how we should say the mantra, and the way we say the mantra is very much the way we are, the way we love, and the way we live day by day. We should say the mantra without impatience, without force or any intention of violence. The purpose of the mantra is not to block out thoughts. It is not a jamming device. If thoughts attack us while meditating, we turn the other cheek. In saying the mantra gently, we learn from him who is gentle and humble of heart. When the mantra leads us into the pure unbounded spaciousness of the mind of Christ, beyond our self-consciousness, into true silence, when the mantra has itself become silent, we will not be timing its duration or recording the experience for later analysis. We will be undergoing transformation. Our lives will, day by day, become the commentary on our prayer. Our prayer will then no longer consist in endlessly commenting on our lives. We will ourselves permanently have become prayer, which is the goal of the Christian way.

Today, as I finish this newsletter in London, our community of meditation around the world is remembering John Main's death. For every birth, there is a death and for every death, a birth. The birth and death of Jesus were events that transformed this universal pattern. We remember the birth of Jesus only because of the life he lives in us through the Resurrection. The light of Resurrection burns up the pattern of death and birth and allows us to see all time and all its recurrent patterns in the present moment of God's care for all creation. The Incarnation transcends all reincarnation.

So, today, close to our remembering the birth of Jesus, we remember the day of death of one of his devoted disciples. We can remember it with gratitude for what it teaches us of the mysteries of accepting the amazing and at times painful punctuality of the Spirit in human affairs. We cannot separate the gift of meditation that has come into so many lives through Fr John's teaching from the man himself. But neither can we identify it with him. What he taught was what the Spirit taught him. He shows us that the best way to receive a gift is to share it. This is the mystery of life which both birth and death teach us.

We wish you a very happy and peaceful new year and pray that it will lead each of us more fully into the life we are born for.

With much love

Laurence

Laurence Freeman, OSB

Letter Six

21 March 1997
Feast of St Benedict

A Backward Glance

Dearest friends,

There is a moment in the *Purgatorio* of Dante when the poet and his guide are toiling up a steep rockface. Dante becomes exhausted and cries out to Virgil for a rest, but he is kindly exhorted to persevere a little further. His "sweet father's" encouragement gives him new strength. Eventually, they reach a ledge where they can both rest and "here we both sat down to face the east, to rest as we surveyed all we had climbed—a backward glance can often lift the heart."

Lent is the Christian season of the backward glance, of recollection, and so of a deeper understanding of where we have reached on the lifelong ascent to the paradiso of our faith. This does not mean living in the past or dwelling neurotically on our sinfulness. The judicious "backward glance" of Lenten mindfulness enhances and strengthens the way we dwell in the present moment which, Jesus reminds us, means also to dwell in his love.

Example teaches us better than words what this means. Being in the presence of someone who dwells in the present moment enlightens the understanding of what the present really is far better than the best book or lecture. When I visited the Dalai Lama at his residence in Dharamsala last month, I was recalled to the meaning of the experience of the present moment which is at the heart of the spiritual practise of every tradition and which is the practical essence of all meditation. As Father John taught: not to think of God but to be with God here and now.

When we arrived to see the Dalai Lama, we soon picked up the disturbance in people's minds caused by the murder of three monks a few days before—an event with external political meanings and another instance of the prolonged and lonely suffering of the Tibetan people in exile from their own land and culture. I knew from previous experience that the Dalai Lama meets people on their own ground, turns toward them and their concerns, and that he does not impose his or his people's needs on his visitors. This is one reason why so many are naturally so attracted to identify with these needs and to help as best they can to resolve the Tibetan tragedy: it is easier to identify with the other-centred than with the self-centred, just as the loving are easier to love than the unloving.

So in my first meeting with the Dalai Lama, we talked about the past, how the Good Heart Seminar of 1994 had borne such fruit for the friendship and the mutual understanding and reverence between Buddhism and Christianity. We talked of the future, of how we could train the vine of our dialogue over the next three years through joint retreats, pilgrimage, and the witness of prayer in places of conflict. Yet, the overwhelming experience of talking of the past and the future with the Dalai Lama was of an expanded awareness of the present moment in which all events have their origin and climb to their consummation. In my next meeting with him, the topics of discussion were not about the calendar but the inner journey. This "spiritual conversation" was in a sense no more spiritual, no more in touch with the present than our earlier one. The present moment is a way of being present to all aspects of life with the same quality of attention and reverence.

The universal attraction and authority of the Dalai Lama have many explanations: his tolerance and compassion, his reminding people to prefer their own religious tradition while recognising their freedom to choose the path which they feel suits them best. Above all, though, he is both loved and admired, as are great teachers in all traditions, because he exhibits in his personality the truths he teaches and he makes these truths seem both humane and accessible to ordinary people. He is fully present to those he is with and to the complex problems of his time while convincing you that he is fully present to himself. I was told how he gives generously of his time and deep attention as he listens to the stories of torture and persecution of Tibetans fleeing to India for safety. His spiritual practise manifestly underlies and informs his work for the world. This, as he well knows and teaches, is not a specifically Buddhist quality, and he is eager to make others aware of how universal and available it is, how powerful a way of peace and reconciliation of human suffering and conflict the experience of the present moment can be.

Living in the present moment is to be in touch with both the centre and the periphery of conscious experience simultaneously, to be as active in time-bound things as we are receptive to the timeless. It is not to be cold or impersonal, nor is it to deny the reality of grief, injustice, and all the forms of suffering in the human or animal worlds. But nor is it to be so overwhelmed and swamped by emotional responses that we contribute more to the sum total of suffering rather than helping to relieve it. The present moment allows the ordinary mind to be engaged in the immediate and also to rest in the longer process by which God brings good out of evil and by which in the end "all will be well." We can approach this ultimate hope that good will triumph over evil either as pious platitude or as heroic engagement with the realities of life, but compassion is the living proof of authentic hope. As the directing and binding force of the process by which all becomes well, a wise and benevolent compassion is the sign, both interior and external, that we are indeed living in the present moment.

The present moment is indescribable and undefinable. It is profoundly silent because it is simply what it is and does not try to express itself except as what it is. For that very reason, we can use many terms to describe it or to try to evoke it. Above all, though, it is caught rather than described, and it is caught from people living in the present. We recognise and understand it most fully by being with them. Much talking about it does not prove that the reality is there. Usually the reverse.

One of the ways the Christian tradition speaks about this reality of the present moment is as life in the spirit. The Spirit breathes freedom beyond the law ("If you are led by the Spirit you are not subject to law" [Gal 5:18]). Spirit produces the many fruits of goodness while also guiding us through daily life by keeping us in touch with the source of our deepest reality ("If the Spirit is the source of our life, let the Spirit also direct its course" [Gal 5:25]). The best expression of the Spirit is the way life is lived, how problems and opportunities are dealt with, and how relationships are respected with the qualities of peace, trust, faith, and joy.

St Benedict teaches us to "make peace your quest and aim." Monasticism (in its many forms) is a universal, transcultural vehicle of this search for the peace of the present moment. It is the peace of God that passes understanding and the search for it is as old as history. Seeking peace is as old as time because it is with the experience of time that we first begin to forget. The more time-bound we become, the more we forget our source and the more it seems that we are traveling away from the source, whereas the present moment reminds us that the source is constant through space and time. All things are in God, and God is in all things. Time divides because it makes us forget that it is only one side of reality's coin. The other side is eternity, not endless time but timelessness. If we restrict ourselves to only the temporal side of the coin, we forget our unity with the Spirit.

Forgetting, we act forgetfully, unmindfully, sinfully. We say the cruel word, we fail to do the kind deed, we communicate the sting of anger rather than the balm of love, we confuse rather than clarify. The most powerful means of recovering from this unhappy and distracted state of suffering is forgiveness. Jesus does not advocate a prolonged concentration or analysis of our sinfulness but a radical and immediate opening of our selves to the giving and receiving of forgiveness. Forgiveness is the shortcut directly into God. The more conditional the forgiving, the more distant God seems to be. The more generously we enter into the cycle and process of forgiveness, the more present God appears. Often, we feel guilty and suffer intensely in the mind because we feel we can't forgive or even don't want to receive forgiveness from those we feel have the greater blame. The guilt of not being able to experience forgiveness is relieved by understanding that forgiveness is a process, a cycle that begins in time and leads into the eternal. Forgiveness is comprised of both giving and receiving.

We forget. Through forgiveness, we remember. This is the daily spiritual practise which occupies the full twenty-four hours of each

day. It is a cycle we repeat countless times each day, even several
times a minute on some difficult occasions. This is not imprecise
because as the great teachers tell us the work of the spirit continues
even in sleep. How we prepare for bed at night is, therefore, important. "Do not let the sun go down on your anger," St Paul advises
and St Benedict, in his concern for the daily practise of the presence
of God in the monk's life, repeats. Saying your night prayers may
not be such a bad way of getting a good night's sleep without the
aid of sedatives. The meditator also knows the gift of repeating the
mantra as he or she goes off to sleep and the joy of waking up with
it still sounding in mind and heart. If it is true that our last thought
determines the way we are born into the timeless, then what our
mind dwells on at night will certainly influence the way we awake
the next day.

The "backward glance" can be a deep remembering of what we
so frequently forget and what forgiveness so quickly and merciful-
ly restores us to. In that glance, however, we are not getting bogged
down in the past or punishing ourselves. We are pursuing the continuous work of forgiveness and reconciliation which is the work of
the Spirit not only in the human realm but on the cosmic scale.

This cycle of spiritual practise unfolds within and with the grace
of the mind of Christ, with whom our lives are inextricably inter-
twined. By his "mind," we do not mean only his intellect but his
sacred heart too: that center of each human person where our different dimensions are reconciled and unified. Here, in the heart-
mind, we are totally and simply ourselves, without masks, without
the anxiety of having to prove ourselves, utterly confident about
who we are, without delusions of grandeur or destructive self-
rejection. The mind of Christ is, therefore, his other-centered self-
knowledge, his authority, and his humility. His mind embraces all
humanity across the sweep of history with a single glance but
bestows a loving look on each individual which brings each to self-
knowledge with the life-changing conviction that we are loved
uniquely and equally. The ego's jealous demand to be loved exclu-
sively is thus dispelled for ever. At the core of Christian faith, then,
is the insight that the individual we know as Jesus of Nazareth, a
great teacher of humanity but one like us, is the same person as the
cosmic Christ, the eternal Word. The Resurrection experience

reveals this identity to us in the glorified humanity of Jesus whose mind fills and contains all that is. Our own journey into self-knowledge, the oft-repeated cycle of forgetting, forgiving, and remembering, makes this insight the central experience of our life.

Living in this faith is life in the present moment, life in the Spirit. A continuous experience of the sacred opens for those who live in this way. Nothing is then meaninglessly profane ever again. Nothing bores us any more. In Eden, everything is sacred and pure. But when we fall into the divided consciousness, as we must in order to attain our highest development, we become entrapped by the maps of purity and the demarcation of the sacred which earlier generations have made. The holy becomes systematized and politicized. If we specify certain times, people, places, and objects as particularly holy, then others can fall victim to our prejudice and be labelled as profane.

Sinners, the handicapped, foreigners become ritually unclean and fair game to be scapegoated. Religion can connive at this by investing holiness as a kind of frozen asset in certain restricted areas. In Ezekiel, there is a long description of how the priests are to prepare for worship in the temple and what special clothes they wear. The passage concludes with this revealing statement: "Before going out to the people in the outer court, they are to remove the clothes they have worn while serving; leaving them in the sacred rooms, they are to put on other clothes, so that they do not by means of their clothing transmit holiness to the people" (Ez 44:19). When it is mapped out like this the "sacred" creates zones of privilege and exclusion.

Jesus defiantly transgressed the maps of the sacred drawn by his religious contemporaries which labeled so many of God's people as impure and excluded them from the feast of the kingdom. He broke the rules by dining with sinners, touching the unclean, treating women as equals, comparing the goodness of the prostitute with the hypocrisy of the priest. In doing so, he was not acting unreligiously. He was affirming the integrity of true religion. The early Christians were intoxicated by what he thus showed them about the holiness of the people of God and the freedom from the Law which holiness bestows. Anyone who reads the gospel in the light of this experience of the sacred sees that holiness is not a privilege or possession but a free-flowing river of the spirit, the self-communicating, and transforming energy of the divine life. There are no boundaries to the sacred.

Compassion is how we most deeply experience this truth of the sacred because compassion is boundless. Our heart opens to the needs of others, regardless of their colour or beliefs. And if we choose to close our hearts to them on these grounds, we forfeit our own humanity and regress further back than even the animal kingdom: our hearts become stone. In compassion, our sense of being an isolated self dissolves. There is a moment of extinction, and then we recover ourselves, free of self-consciousness in the other. We are then most fully living in the present moment, not trying to experience the experience, but one with the flow of the spirit through time and space. When we awaken to God inside the consciousness of another, spontaneously willing and working for their good, we are most truly living in Christ.

A recent visit I made to a dying woman in hospital taught me much about this. She was not an easy person with whom to visit or speak. Her level of anger and bitterness at life, God, and the church could become very high. She blamed everything for giving her, as she saw it, nothing, an unfulfilled life without ecstasy. She had obeyed all the rules governing the sacred and the pure, and she felt cheated. I had brought her communion, and she made it very clear she was not interested in receiving this sacrament of the church to which she had such violently ambivalent feelings. It seemed to be wrong to try to persuade her otherwise. We talked through her obsessive complaints several times, and I rose to go. She held me back and asked if I wanted to read one of her poems. Rummaging in her locker, I found some handwritten poems which were too difficult for me to decipher, so I asked her to choose and read me one.

I was not expecting anything so beautiful as what she read. It seemed to be incredible that such sensitivity and beauty could come from such an angry and pained mind. I was visibly moved, and she was watching my reactions carefully. When she saw them, her mind cleared for an instant, the real person she was shone through in a smile of immense tenderness and nobility in the face of her disappointed life and painful death. For me, this was a moment of the communion she had earlier refused. I left convinced that Christ had been present to her through the sacredness of her art and the holy communion of her self-communication to another person. The only map of the sacred is the cosmos itself.

We enter the present moment through the stilling of the mind. Many things can achieve this, and anything that does so is sacred. To make this stillness more than a brief encounter with reality but a way of life, we need a regular practise of stillness, such as meditation provides. This we must then come to love, and be deeply devoted to the path of our teacher's initiation, not as something we choose as spiritual consumers but as what we are chosen. In accepting that, we taste the liberty of being that the Spirit anoints us with. False perceptions of the world disappear, as Ramana Maharshi said, when the mind becomes still. This does not mean the world or our down-to-earthness disappears.

Quite the reverse occurs. We realise insight into the simple real nature of ordinary things and moments. The ordinary becomes sacred through its suchness. It is as if the sense of taste or smell, vision, or touch is suddenly restored, and we had hardly guessed we had lost it. Contemplation, as Aquinas said, is the simple enjoyment of the truth. The experience of the present moment does not end with this sharpened sensory awareness of the is-ness or suchness of things: the scent of the rose or of springtime earth, the taste of an orange that recalls our childhood. The senses, as the Christian sacraments remind us, are deeply involved in our sense of the sacred; but in the present moment, we sense something beyond the external senses: some quality within and beyond the suchness of things in space and moments of time. We sense the ground of being itself, that ground with which Jesus knew himself to be one and from which he knew his being directly derived.

> The soul that moves in the world of the senses and yet keeps the senses in harmony free from attraction and aversion finds rest in stillness. (Bhagavad Gita 2:64)

> God's invisible attributes, his everlasting power and deity, have been visible, ever since the world began, to the eye of reason in the things he has made. (Rom 1:20)

In the present moment, we experience a fullness of life that liberates us from the fear of death. Rooted in the present, we can see the rising and falling of things, which is the process of dying that renews and deepens life. Death is an abstraction we fear. Dying is a daily reality we can face and accept. Thoughts and feelings are born and die in the mind every moment, just as the cells of our bodies are continuously dying and being replaced. Sleep draws us into the dying of each day and our rebirth in new hope the next. The biological and psychological phases of our life similarly teach us that life is not opposed to death but is a compound of death and birth. Life is not negated by death. It is only a habit of language, the meaning we give to words, that would have us believe so.

Lent and Easter invite us to see the sacredness of dying and the blissfulness of life in relation to each other. The gospel stories that we re-read so intensely in this season give an apparently disproportionate amount of space to the passion and death of Jesus. Only if we have lost a sense of the sacred could we regard this as morbid. The death of Jesus teaches us definitively everything that his words and miracles communicate; it helps us to hear his timeless words and reflect on his life's actions with the enlightenment of understanding his Resurrection bestows. His disciples once wondered privately what Jesus meant by "rising from the dead." They were frightened to ask because it stirred their primal fear of death.

We today can explore his meaning without fear because the achievement of the Resurrection is the casting out of that basic fear of death that haunts the human mind. To explore what rising from the dead means is to enter it for ourselves, to know in our experience of the present moment that dying and birth are contained in life. We learn from the stillness that meditation itself is, as it leads us into the present moment in all our daily activities, that life is sacred with the holiness, not of manmade maps, but of the Spirit without boundaries.

The present moment is not measured by the watch on our wrist but by our mindful watching of every action. It is not at 10:50 A.M. in Florence with the Sunday bell of the cathedral chiming over the sunlit city as I sit now typing these words in San Miniato where Christians have worshipped for more than a thousand years. It is not the moment now when you are reading these words and wondering why it takes so many words to say something so simple. It is not the Dalai Lama waiting patiently and urgently, joyful and suffering in the foothills of the Himalayas, a few tantalising miles from the country where he was born and where his people and religion are being destroyed as the world discusses trade agreements.

The present moment is the mind of Christ in which writer and reader, now and then, Buddhist and Christian, male and female, Jew and Greek, slave and free meet and join him in his blissful journey into the one source to which every birth and death always point. To know that moment of Christ is to know what rising from the dead means. It is to be empowered for what life asks of us and invites us into each day.

With much love

Laurence

Laurence Freeman, OSB

Letter Seven

6 August 1997
Feast of the Transfiguration

Friendship

Dearest friends,

The Community's first "School for Teachers"—teachers of meditation—was held in Florence this June. Thirty-five people, ranging in age from mid-twenties to mid-seventies, came together from ten countries on five continents. At the beginning, everybody already knew somebody, but nobody knew everybody. Something happened on the first evening which I have often noticed when a disparate group of meditators gets together, though you can never guarantee it will happen: everybody recognised each other.

People intuited that, even if they could not say yet that they were friends, there was evidently friendship among them. Once that is sensed and trusted, the rest is simply a matter of time and of chance: the time, for example, it takes for the psyche, even when it has been disarmed of much of its caution and suspicion, to form bonds of memory and shared experience with others; and the chance of who you sit next to or whose coat you walk off with by mistake, whose eye you catch when the group is laughing, what it is that conversation shows you have unexpectedly in common.

We had come together to discuss better ways of sharing the gift of meditation with others around the world. So we had a clear and sincere common goal and a strong bond in our thankful commitment to meditation. We also had a high degree of personal individuality and self-awareness and a very broad spectrum of gifts and temperaments. If we had been meeting to discuss marketing strategy for a new product and if our meetings had only been to talk about that, I think our initial intuition of pre-existent friendship would not have been realised as richly as it eventually was. The friendships in the end proved so rich not because we were only talking about meditation but because we were actually doing the work of silence together, morning, midday, and evening. Things change in silence. People change. A unity of friendship came into being, nourished on all the unpredictable diversity among us.

Each day began with meditation as we sat around a pool of water lilies in the elegant gardens of the Villa Agape, near our meditation centre at San Miniato overlooking Florence where most participants were staying. It was a beautiful spot which we came to love. The pond was a world within a world with its own complex interdependencies and delights: the flowers opening and closing at the beginning and end of each day; the visiting busy bees and iridescent dragonflies steering their paths through the heavy insect traffic; the frogs clinging smilingly to the edge of the pond, and their tadpoles visibly maturing. Around the pond, the Americans, Australians, Asians, and Europeans did the work most natural to them as human beings, the work of becoming clear-minded and loving-hearted on behalf of each other and of all creation. And beyond us were the tireless choirs of birds, the prowling convent cats, the swaying sharp-pointed cypresses. And further on, the streets of Florence already were filling with businesslike traders and dutiful tourists. And beyond that, the measureless world whose unity and friendship we can only imagine holding together in Christ.

When your starting-point for looking at the mystery of the world is the security and delight of friendship, it is not difficult to see the world as an infinite interwoven succession of spheres of friendship. Discovering the world and understanding one's self then become a single task, the seeing and naming of the invisible affinities of friendship which tie us to everything and everything to us. If human trust and companionship is not the point from which we begin, the world never seems such a friendly place.

Our confidence in the importance of meditation for the modern world was, therefore, rooted in a very personal experience. We knew we were friends because we meditated; in other words, we were not meditating together just because we were friends. Meditation was not just a shared interest. If that had been the case, we would probably not have been trying to see ways to share the gift of meditation with others. We knew meditation was worth sharing because we had seen how it revealed in human and in toughly down-to-earth ways that even strangers with much to divide them are basically friends. Friendship is part of our true nature, however much we may forget, deny, or abuse it. As frogs, dragonflies, and water lilies shared a common home in the pond, human beings continually come home, to themselves, to each other, in God. Meditation, as we were reminded when we discussed the title for an introductory seminar we were working on, is about *Coming Home.*

At the Monte Oliveto Retreat two weeks later, the participants took the theme of spiritual friendship for deeper reflection at the conferences and discussion times. Our special guide was St Aelred of Rievaulx. The twelfth-century English monk believed so much in the theological and spiritual reality of friendship that he went so far as to paraphrase St John's "God is love" as "God is friendship." Aelred explored the Christian meaning of friendship with us within a tradition of thought that long predates Christianity.

One of the oldest ideas in the human mind concerns friendship. It is as if when human consciousness first woke up, the first and most fascinating things it noticed were the human need and capacity for relationship that went beyond the bounds observable in the natural world.

> The good person is related to his friend as he is to himself since the friend is another himself. (Aristotle)

From the time of the earliest thinkers, therefore, friendship was considered inseparable from goodness. Friendship is a supreme human virtue: both a strength and a pride. Friendship cannot be cultivated or enjoyed for bad ends or among people who are united in a bad cause. There may be honour among thieves but not friendship. If a friend is "another myself," it is because in friendship the essential goodness of human nature is—eventually—permitted to become fully visible. Friendship is a way of seeing myself in others and others in myself. The Desert Fathers and Mothers saw the archetype of the monk in this way. For them, the monk was, by virtue of his detachment from all, in union with all. The monk is everyone's friend. Before Christianity, the same holographic vision of reality was expressed in the Isa Upanishad: *Who sees all beings in his own Self, and his own Self in all beings, loses all fear.*

When the classical philosophers came to write about friendship, they agreed that certain conditions were necessary and others were propitious for the full development of friendship. It was seen to be impossible, for example, to be friends with someone you fear.

Aelred, following his classical mentor Cicero, also understood that you cannot be friends with someone without knowing it. Friendship is by nature conscious and might even be called a form of consciousness. Therefore, friendship, like other forms of love, has to be declared in some way or other, and there is a certain kind of delight just in articulating it. For Jesus, it was his joy to tell us of his friendship with us:

> I have spoken thus to you, so that my joy may be in you, and your joy complete. This is my commandment: love one another, as I have loved you. There is no greater love than this, that a man should lay down his life for his friends. You are my friends, if you do what I command you. I call you servants no longer; a servant does not know what his master is about. I have called you friends, because I have disclosed to you everything I have learned from my Father. (Jn 15:11–15)

In declaring his friendship to humanity, Jesus opens a new way of seeing God and therefore, as God is "all in all," a new way of seeing everything. Friendship becomes a way of relating to Jesus and to the Father and, therefore, to each other. In this perspective, because we cannot love the invisible God without loving our visible neighbour, any one relationship in our life contains every other relationship. What this means is that by loving one person we are embarking on an endless journey into the infinite interdependencies of the universe, a journey whose purpose is to lead us to love every person. Only when friendship is all-inclusive will we be able to say we love God with our whole heart and mind.

For the Christian, Jesus is a supreme teacher of this mystery. But he is also the key to the mystery, the path through the labyrinth. He is the single person who expands into a universality beyond our imagination of him even while we come to know and love him. As he expands in and among us, disclosing who he is, we deepen our friendship with him. His delight in our friendship sparks off ours, and our joy grows and grows through many deaths of the ego until it bursts all the constraining forms of our identity, and we love as he loves and as God loves.

Every relationship is a way of seeing. Friendship is a way of seeing truthfully and clearly. Today, our interest in friendship is predominantly, sometimes narrowly, psychological. Because we are so preoccupied about relationships, rightly thinking of them as the sacred ground of our lives, we can become frightened at the way relationships fail and break down. We can even be frightened at what we perceive as our incapacity to make or sustain relationships at all. In classical times, it was thought that one of the goals of good civil legislation was to protect the influence of the bonds of friendships in all the networks of society because it was seen that the health of friendship ultimately determined not only the quality of life but also the exercise of justice in society. We may be a long way from enjoying that sense of the connection between public and private values. But we may find a way forward through the confusion of modern culture by seeing friendship in more than the perspective offered by ego-based psychology. Perhaps in friendship we can find the key for a unified and unifying moral vision which has been so disastrously shattered. But, in addition to its moral meaning, there are theological, spiritual, and mystical spheres to human friendship which the declaration of friendship by Jesus invites us to understand.

> And so I should say that friendship takes its beginning from our very nature rather than from our sense of inadequacy— from an inclination of the heart and feelings of affection rather than from what advantages we can get from it. (Cicero)

To understand friendship better, we need to think rationally about its emotional currents. St Aelred is no sentimentalist, even though he speaks movingly about the "sweetness" of friendship and its delights. He knows that sweetness becomes cloying and can turn sour if it is pursued immoderately or irrationally. To allow our full capacity for friendship to develop and our individual friendships to flourish, we must, he advises, embark upon them as clear-headedly as possible. This means firstly being aware that friendship is natural. In the story of Creation, God's first concern for Man after making him is not to leave us alone even in the garden of earthly delights. God is anxious to find us a suitable companion:

> It is not good for Man to be alone; I shall make a partner suited to him. (Gn 2:18)

God tried to find this partner in the animal world but eventually had to put Adam into deep sleep, remove one of his ribs, and thus make out of his flesh and blood "another himself." In the human realm, therefore, the need for friendship seems to precede even the need for biological survival. And the friendship of Adam and Eve did not spoil their friendship with God but rather fulfilled and celebrated it. One of the universal pre-requisites of friendship is equality between friends. Genesis shows the necessary complementarity of male and female as the foundation of their friendship. Eden was a world of friendship, sphere within sphere of harmonious interweaving relationship, the universal shalom between God, Man, and Nature.

Because friendship is natural, it is also necessary. No one would ever choose to live without it, Aristotle thought. If you are happy and prosperous, you want friends to share your good times. If you are poor or in pain, you need friends to help you out. If you are young, you need friends to form you for adult life in the world. When you are old, you need friends to prepare you for death.

As with the mystery of time, we all know what friendship is but no one can explain it adequately. So, let's say it is "reciprocated good-will." That is to say, wishing well to another for their own sake. It must also be conscious, and then it becomes contagious. We are naturally attracted to friendship. We are attracted, for example, to people we may not know but who have shown themselves to be good friends to others, who are loyal and trustworthy, who are open about themselves, and who demonstrate reverence in all the friendships of their life, even with those who have died. People who have proved themselves good friends become the "good company" we like to be in and close to.

Because friendship is so naturally attractive and necessary for the good life, how can it ever be truly selfless? Aren't we always in it for what we get out of it? In a sense, yes. But we soon learn that we only get out of it what we put into it. To set out on the path of friendship (part of what we call "commitment" today) is to begin a novitiate, which as St Aelred knew, involves many trials and humiliations and much suffering before a true love of self and others can be achieved. We soon learn that there are different kinds of friendships and that we must be able to discern these distinctions because "friends are most at odds when they are not friends in the way they think they are."

According to Aelred and the tradition in which he is writing, there is, firstly, utilitarian friendship in which the partners involved are getting advantages for themselves out of it. In business or politics, these friendships ebb and flow, moving in and out of integrity. This kind of friendship fades with the usefulness of the friend. In any case, St Ambrose in his contribution to the subject, says friendship is not a trade but a thing of beauty full of grace.

Another kind of friendship springs primarily from the pleasure gained from the other's presence, and so it will fade with the decline of passion. This, too, has many forms, the most obvious aspect being that based on mutual sexual pleasure. Extra-marital affairs or promiscuity can also, however, be typical manifestations within this type of friendship that both Christian and classical thinkers regarded as suspect. Like utilitarian friendships, these kinds are very varied and complex, and they all can lead to a certain degree into a "spiritual friendship," whose dignity consists in becoming a way of participating in the friendship that is God.

Spiritual friendship, then, is the most real. It can only grow in a maturing atmosphere of trust and a shared love of transcendent goodness. It will only grow through the hard tests time will inevitably impose on it. Partners in such friendships will have learned how to love themselves and so be capable of entrusting their most private selves to each other in full confidence. Even though Aelred makes high theological claims for friendship, seeing it as beginning, advancing, and reaching perfection in Christ, he insists that a high degree of self-awareness must accompany the relationship throughout its life. Friendship must begin and continue with a process of selection and testing that precedes a rational and moderate admission of the friend to deepening degrees of trust.

He places great emphasis on the sacredness of personal trust and shared confidences. Few things, he knew from experience, are more devastating than the betrayal of friendship's trust or the revealing to others of a secret entrusted as an act of faith and love.

Being in friendship is to risk one's life. Indeed, it is to "lay down one's life." A monk with whom Aelred discusses friendship in his treatise *De Amicitia Spirituale* is more reserved and cautious than Aelred. "Why risk so much? Why not embark on friendship for its companionship and sweetness but always hold something back so that you protect yourself from betrayal?" For Aelred, this is the voice not so much of reason as of a half-hearted love of the gospel itself. But this warning about the high stakes of friendship alerts us to a fact which no reflection about friendship can ignore: the shadow-side of friendship which we most ordinarily experience as betrayal or jealousy. We cannot understand spiritual friendship, or its place in the gospel life, without coming to terms with its shadow.

For Kierkegaard, this shadow is expressed as jealousy, possessiveness, and exclusivity. Betrayal in friendship is a sign that there is nothing essentially Christian about it: "If anyone thinks that by falling in love or by finding a friend he has learned Christian love, he is in profound error."

His chilling denunciation of friendship as a subtly deceptive form of self-love and his even chillier exaltation of the Christian alternative of "love of neighbour" is very persuasive. Bring the demand of love of a "neighbour," he says, between two "friends" and you will find jealousy. The supposedly generous gift of self to a friend is no more than the highest concentration of egotism because it always demands to be reciprocated.

To understand the friendship with himself that Jesus offers humanity in and through the experience of friendship with one another demands that we face the shadow that Jesus himself endured: to understand fully the light of Jesus we must also understand the shadow Judas casts over his life. At the Last Supper, Jesus announced that he was going to be betrayed, and the disciple Jesus loved asked him by whom? Jesus indicated Judas by giving him the piece of bread and then, "As soon as Judas received it Satan entered him. Jesus said to him 'Do quickly what you have to do.' No one at the table understood what he meant by this. . . . As soon as Judas received the bread he went out. It was night" (Jn 13:27).

The passage is made haunting by the horrific contrasts of light and shade: the beloved disciple and the friend-turned-traitor, the Eucharistic bread becoming a sign of treachery, the warm, well-lit interior security of the friendly meal and the dark outside to which the false friend is sent. Most horrifying of all is that no gospel gives a clear motive for Judas's betrayal. Yet, no reader of the gospel can fail to feel a strange sympathy or identification with Judas. On deeper reading, in fact, you cannot ignore the odd sense of intimacy between him and Jesus in their shared knowledge of what he was to do. But when we remember that all the apostles except for the beloved disciple were later to betray or abandon Jesus, we begin to sense how much Judas symbolises a tendency at work in everyone of us.

Maybe friendship is natural and necessary and capable of bringing us into friendship with the God who is friendship, but there is a terrible and real part of us that denies and rejects that. We deny God's first statement about the human person that it is not good for us to be alone. The Shadow declares "I want to be apart; I am alone." I heard this recently at an Alcoholics Anonymous meeting when a young man was describing his slow recovery, a new job, a new start in his marriage with his loving and loyal wife. He spoke in a calm quiet voice about the overpowering urge he was struggling with to get rid of his wife and of all other ties just so that he could go back to the drink.

As the shadow's darkness deepens, its self-destructive rage metamorphoses from anger into hatred. It desires not only to inflict pain but to deprive others even of their capacity to feel pain, to destroy them. Not all of us have the alcoholic's shockingly clear self-awareness. And though not many of us can face the shadow in ourselves, even during its milder attacks, every marriage, friendship, and community does suffer from the shadow of isolation and fear and its capacity for rage and hatred. Perhaps it is created in the psyche by the belief that we are not loved and its accompanying nightmare that we are unlovable. It is this same shadow, which has its roots perhaps in the most unconscious of urges, the instinct to survive, which can insanely see all others as a threat to our existence.

The "shadow of friendship" has many manifestations: the ethnic cleansing of Serbia, the double-life of infidelity lived by a marriage-partner, the betrayal of a friend's confidence, behaviour destructive of trust and respect in community, and, more subtly, the reasoned but fearful refusal to risk the stronger consciousness of intimacy. It seems to me that all this highlights the spiritual significance of friendship as a sacrament of the divine love for humanity. If friendship does indeed lead to God, as Aelred says it does, it is not so surprising, is it, that the breakdown of friendship should lead us to Satan? If Eden was the garden of friendship, hell is understandable as the pit where friends are lost and betrayed.

What then does the shadow mean for friendship? Should we politely avoid friendship to save ourselves from the shadow? The problem then, however, is that the shadow is in us anyway because we are all wounded to some degree by the experience of rejection and the feeling of unlovableness. Only friendship will expose and neutralize it. Once we have owned up to being the source of the shadow, we can face the fact that we do cast shadows on our friends. Then we are free from the unconscious need to demonise others as we withdraw our projections from them and see the faults in our own personalities and behaviour. We can begin to guess what we are up to and even anticipate the shadow's appearances and flare-ups. This is a meaning perhaps of Jesus' knowing so clearly in John's Gospel how and by whom he would be betrayed.

The only way to deal with our shadow is to walk in it. We cannot walk on a sunny day anywhere without the company of our own shadow (except in the still-point of noonday!). The shadow will be with us until the end of our life. However, we cannot walk alone in it for long without despair or self-destruction. Friendship, deriving from and returning to the friendship of God which Jesus shares with every human being, allows us to walk in the shadow without fear. The only way to endure and cure a friend's shadow is to walk in it with great consciousness. To walk in the shadow of another is to suffer, even to be mortally wounded. This can be so real that we should never underestimate the power of the shadow for sheer destruction.

There is one overpowering reason, however, why we are able to face and embrace our shadow. It is that Jesus who is the light of the world has walked in the human shadow. He has borne the burden of the shadow we call sin, and he allowed it to destroy him. But in that destruction, he remained awake and went even deeper than the "night" of his betrayal and death into the underworld from which the shadow arises. His descent into hell and his ascension into heaven means that there is no shadow which we can now encounter which has not been graced by his light. There is much terrible darkness still in the world and in human relationships. But there never was absolute darkness. In the worst shadows of life, we meet the crucified and risen one.

This conviction of faith does not absolve us from suffering, but it empowers us to embrace whatever must be endured. Aelred said that we endure and cure each other's faults in friendship. St Benedict, before him, urged us to bear one another's burdens. The friendship of Christ for us continues to do that until our time is ended. We should not make any friends, therefore, unless we want to walk in their shadow and to see them walking in ours. The "testing" of friends, which St Aelred advises, is perhaps only a way of compassionately seeing whether we can mutually endure (and so cure) our respective shadows! If we can, then by walking together like the disciples on the road to Emmaus, we can experience "sweetly" how Christ reveals himself within our friendship.

> And thus a friend praying to Christ on behalf of his friend and, for his friend's sake, desiring to be heard by Christ, directs his attention with love and longing to Christ; then it sometimes happens that quickly and imperceptibly the one love passes over into the other and coming into contact with the sweetness of Christ himself the friend begins to taste his sweetness and to experience his charm. (St Aelred)

Aelred's theology of human friendship suggests the profound non-duality of our oneness with Christ. Through a spiritual understanding of friendship, we can see how the wisdom of the Tao and of Advaita are present in the Christian experience of sin and death, grace and salvation, cross and resurrection. In the light of this experience, there is no reason to avoid the shadow and every reason to have the courage to embrace it. Although it is the enemy of friendship, it can, after much loving and wisdom, be made a friend. The few saints we may meet in our life show us this by their shadowless translucence, their personal integration.

How do we walk in our own shadow while allowing it to be enlightened? Meditation is the great teacher here. By saying the mantra with faith and love in the friendly presence of Christ, we are better able to embrace and integrate the enemy within us so as to make it our servant rather than a tyrant over us. In due course, it can even become our friend and help us to see that our true self has always been and can only be a Friend. The longer we meditate, the more we realise how much the mantra itself is a friend. Like all friends, once selected, we must learn to be faithful to it. Eventually, it breaks through the shadow of the ego and merges into friendship with the Word that is Jesus and so into union, into friendship, with all. It is not so surprising that the fruits of meditation are best perceived at work in our relationships and in our very capacity for friendship in all its forms.

En route, we learn that fellow pilgrims are friends. We see that friends are other "ourselves" because in relationship with them we are one with the true self in which there are no divisions. We see how Christ, who has chosen us for his friends and tests us so that he can admit us into the friendship that is God, is the doorway into friendship with God.

The image of the mixed group of meditators sitting around the water lily pool captured for me something of the beauty of what Aelred means by spiritual friendship.

Another image that speaks of the vast mystery of Christ's friendship with humanity struck me one day during the School as I was walking up the steps from the crypt of the Abbey Church of San Miniato. Half-way up the stairs, I saw an uninterrupted view of the length of the basilica ending at the open door of the church. A few inches higher and I would have seen through to the panoramic view of Florence that San Miniato commands from its position on the hill, which draws breath from the already breathless pilgrims. But from where I was standing at that moment, I could see only the clearest bright sky framed strongly by the dark door frame and the dark simple interior of the church. There was nothing to see except the full clear emptiness of the sky outside, pure light framed by the interior shade.

Jesus once described himself as a doorway through which we pass into the boundlessness of God. He teaches us this through his friendship with us and through all human friendship.

With much love

Laurence

Laurence Freeman, OSB

Photos of the School for Teachers may be viewed at the WCCM web site: www.wccm.org.

Letter Eight

18 October 1997
Feast of St Luke

Holiness

Dearest friends,

The prophet Mohammed said that people are asleep. When they die, they awake. And so, we all should learn to die before we die. The deaths of others are often the simplest teachers of this truth, which, like most obvious truths, is subject to a daily forgetting. But when someone close to us dies, we are painfully reminded—the pain of grieving is part of it—that we are mortal and that we should not waste the time we are given. When Mother Teresa died, the world grieved. Even those who had never met her felt the pain of her leaving the world in which she had been such a pure, passionate flame of selfless love. All those who had met her even briefly must have remembered the moment as one of the most truly significant of their lives.

I remembered the first time I met her, when I was celebrating Mass very early one morning with her sisters in Bombay. When I was introduced to her afterward and she was told I was going shortly to Calcutta, she said she would like her sisters to hear about meditation and asked if I would give them some talks. When we discussed times and dates, she did not hesitate to begin suggesting alterations to my schedule. It took some effort not to be overwhelmed and taken over. She spoke with the kind of impetuous certainty that makes you feel either very confident or very sceptical.

You feel toward some people of strong personality that you could be swept off your feet and easily made to feel resentful later. Perhaps you should dig your heels in and refuse to be influenced. Or perhaps the force in the person is one that would sweep you faster toward the place you are already moving toward. Meeting such power is a judgement call. Yet, Mother Teresa was so open about her wishes and clear-minded about how she wanted them carried out that I did not feel the object of manipulation. There was passion in her will-power but also a humorous detachment from her own strong ego which made you feel your freedom was respected. If you opposed her, you would not have been making an enemy. When I said I could not change my flights and other engagements, she did not seem irritated or impatient as a bully or a manipulator would, but quite reasonably looked at other available times.

There was also a high-ranking Indian soldier at the Mass who was eager to meet her. It was amusing to see him, tall and bemedalled in his military uniform, towering above her, small and plain in her sari, and to notice the far greater force of her personality over his as he tried, good-naturedly, to patronise her. When he tried to embrace her as he left, she fended him off with the deftness of a judo master. Though she was not a manipulator, she would not be manipulated.

What I, like what most others who met her, remember about Mother Teresa is the extraordinary quality of direct and total attention she would give you while you were with her. There was no overt religious content to the attention. You were not being preached at. Later as the experience of her attention found its permanent place in your mental world, you realised you were not being paid attention to by just another individual personality. But that through her you were being looked at by Christ. Sensing that, you can begin to distinguish between the personal foibles, the unredeemed egotism, and even the sinfulness within those in whom true holiness also radiates.

St Anthony of the Desert once spoke to his monks about the judgement day which they would each confront in their moment of death. He told them that they would not be judged on how far they had become like him, or like any of the other great masters of the desert, but to what degree they had become truly themselves. Holiness as the goal and meaning of human existence may be a quality we recognise in many different people, a scent of which we are conscious. There is a universality about holiness which cuts across age, culture, and religious boundaries. It is not the product of a particular brand of training, and however much individual ideologies try to claim it for themselves, it defies any attempt to label it. What is universal about its nature is that it becomes perceptible in people who have become themselves. Holiness is the presence of God in the human beings who are God's image. Becoming holy is then simply the conscious reunion of image and original.

So much of life seems to fade from memory. Problems that torment us, pleasures that thrill us, plans that absorb us totally, and inconsolable griefs that seem they will end our life are all tempered by time. There are other experiences, often not so emotionally overwhelming at the time they occur, which do not fade. We remember these epiphanies of full consciousness most deeply because they become part of us. In the often quiet and modest way in which they happened, they peeled away some of the usual obscuring layers and revealed to us what we are truly like, who we really are. In this awakening, there was no great thunderclap, no mystical headlines. But it was real news. Something whose news-worthiness did not fade with the morning papers. These are the earthquakes of stillness which rearrange the landscape of our lives, the hurricanes of silence which change the way we listen and speak for the rest of our lives. We remember the moments of such epiphanies because, for some reason we can never explain, we were ready for them when they happened, even though they took us by surprise. And we were awake when they happened. Probably, without realising it, we had just died.

I remember, for example, as a boy coming home from school, how I would often stand at a shop window displaying what were for me irresistibly gorgeous packages of foreign stamps. One day, an older friend of my family walked past and interrupted my rapt contemplative gaze to greet me. The next day, as I was standing at the same window as usual on my way home, the same person walked by and, with an amused expression, asked me if I had been there since yesterday. Something indescribable but utterly familiar flashed on within me which is with me to this day—a self-awareness, a being taken by surprise but without fear, the knowledge that we exist in the universe of others as well as in our own. Whatever the way we describe such moments—and they are very common because they punctuate our growth in consciousness—they are the proofs we need that we are real. That we exist. And when that proof has sunk deeply enough into us, we begin to find the meaning of existence as a growth in holiness.

Holiness is perhaps like music. It is indescribable except in its own language. But it is a universal language that can be heard and appreciated by all people. In a society like ours where religious language and traditions have become such a specialised dialect rather than a common and unifying language, this music of holiness is especially important. Holiness unites us in friendship and in a common belief in the core goodness of humanity. Perhaps because of this, there is a great search for holiness in our supposedly desacralised world. Because people do not go to church, because they don't understand the things that agitate religious people so sorely—like their dogmatic disputes, their controversies over the equality of women, their hostility to people of other communities of faith—this does not mean that they have lost a sense of the sacred or their longing to hear the music of holiness played.

At our meditation centre in London, we witnessed a vivid portrayal of this in August after the tragic death of Princess Diana. We are a few hundred yards from Kensington Palace, which as her London home became the focal point for the extraordinary expression of grief that followed the news of her death. Within days, the lawns in front of the palace had become a shrine as colourful as any in India. The normally reticent English—for whom religious feeling is rarer than their already rare expressions of emotion—had initiated the global canonisation of a public personality whose exposure of her most private experiences and feelings had evidently implanted her as a living symbol in a vast multitude of individual minds. The media, always ready to make and exploit a profitable story, seemed on this occasion genuinely surprised and were themselves carried along by the force of this eruption of the collective unconscious. Characteristic of our instant and impatient culture, the media like everyone else, including those at the meditation centre, was interpreting the true and ultimate meaning of the phenomenon even before it was over.

The flowers, photographs, candles, and prayers that expressed the sense of the sacred in the public grief over Diana's death had a religious language. But the churches who were called in to try to respond to the mass emotion often seemed unable to comprehend it. A few, coming to the moment from a deeper spiritual awareness like Cardinal Hume, did seem to understand and so were able to offer a true and useful spiritual insight into what was happening and to what so many were obviously so genuinely and deeply feeling. When, in the midst of it, Mother Teresa died, the symbolic overload seemed complete. Photographs of the two together were widely displayed to enhance the process which had already gathered such momentum around Princess Diana. Amid the ensuing torrent of instant commentary and interpretation, one thing was very clear, and it was soon repeated in the unexpected multitude of youth who flocked to hear the pope in Paris and Rio de Janeiro: the hunger for evidence of holiness is profound. And it is the hunger that cannot be satisfied by anything less than the real thing.

Media events lack profundity. They can be "experiences" in themselves, but they are rarely among the experiences that stay with us as part of ourselves for the rest of our lives. The media's opportunistic hunger for the novelty of news rarely allows them to deepen the first impressions they make. Yet, the media is a force in our lives and so must be reckoned a contributive part of our spirituality. As we have seen so recently, the media can help to generate the symbols and communicate the feelings and insights which have a genuinely important role to play in our spiritual unfolding and sense of sharing the same spiritual journey with others. The media has the power to trivialise, distort, and exploit, but they can also reflect to us across our divergent cultures and faiths how deeply interdependent we are. Like any other purveyor of strong experience, the media can become addictive. We can grow dependent on the highs the newsmakers feed us many times a day. In this sense, the media might be compared with the mystery religions of the ancient world. Although the modern media abhor mystery and want everything proclaimed from the housetops, they also initiate people into certain forms of knowledge and use carefully orchestrated strong experiences to do so.

The early Christian theologians had to contend with the attraction of these initiatory cults as well as with the many forms of gnosticism. In some ways, gnosticism (from the Greek *gnosis* meaning *knowledge*) was a great over-simplifier. It saw a radical dualism of good and evil, matter and spirit, at the heart of reality. It may seem a bit far-fetched to compare these ancient gnostic cults with the modern media, but they share something in common: the media, like the gnostics, prefer sharp profiles and oppositions. The media find the subtleties of truth difficult to popularise. They prefer saints and devils ranged against each other, and the newsmakers can decide exactly how the roles can be changed as a new spin is given to an old story. In their opposition to these distorting dualities, the early Christians asserted that it was not just by initiation into gnosis that we are saved. Experiential knowledge is not even a precondition for salvation as it is in the various forms of spiritual elitism which limit the number of the saved to a predestined few. We are saved by faith. The faith is already charged with the knowledge we need. As Julian of Norwich said, we are allowed to know only what we need to know. We are saved—made holy—because we can believe wholeheartedly in more than we remember having experienced.

The danger of saying this is that it may suggest that faith and experience are unconnected. It can lead to a religious mentality in which experience is even suspect or avoided in favour of orthodox conformity. But faith is faith in the experience of reality and in the authenticity of our own experience. To have *faith* in someone is to experience their reality, even if not fully. To be faithful is to grow in the *experience* of that to which we are faithful. To meditate is to follow a way that opens up into a spirituality which is simultaneously a way of faith and of experience.

Faith is orientated toward ultimate reality. This orientation is what gives coherence to our values and helps to prioritise them in daily life. Without this orientation and the attitudes it creates, we cannot live with a sense of meaning. But ultimate reality cannot be made into the peak experience of a media event. We cannot validly identify any of our experiences of enlightenment with enlightenment itself. If you can understand it, said St Augustine, it isn't God! That is why it is so important that we don't become fixated on any blissful experiences that we may pass through in meditation or try to reproduce them. It is salutary to remember that our posture is probably more important than our transient experiences. The posture of body *and* mind stabilises and balances us in a wakefulness of pure attention. Posture combats the inherent laziness of undisciplined, random mental activity—in a sense, even our anxieties and compulsions are kinds of laziness. And in the stillness of an alert, total posture, we enter the stillness of God which reveals the true nature of our selves. In stillness, clarity of consciousness and purity of heart unfold as the most natural things in the world.

Good posture is a matter of habit. Good habit. In this, it is like holiness. The holiness in Mother Teresa that one remembers for the rest of one's life was also the fruit of regular practise and became so much a part of her that it was her. Her holiness and her abiding influence in the world were not the result of particular grand gestures or great experiences such as the media adore. It flowed from the countless small acts of kindness which constituted her knowledge of Christ and her adoration of Christ in the poorest of the poor, the neglected and anonymous, the un-newsworthy. And the meaning of these myriad small gestures of love (a glass of water to the thirsty, a scrap of clothing for the naked, a visit to the housebound, a moment wasted with the abandoned) is that they were as habitual as her prayer. Her acts of attention to the poor or to the countless visitors she met every day were the same habit as her act of attention to Christ within herself at prayer, in the Eucharist, within her sisters and their community life.

Everything depends on what we have become habituated to. If we are habituated to TV and soap-opera, that is how we will perceive the world. We will, like the media, reduce the most solemn moments of life to the parameters of the melodramatic and sensational. We will turn conversation into gossip. Criticism will become revenge. Prayer becomes a matter of peak experiences, the pursuit of the merely miraculous. It will not be until our own imminent death, and maybe not even then, that we will understand the true seriousness and joy of our existence. The ultimate reality of holiness is built upon regular practise. Regularity is by definition unexceptional. This does not mean, as a culture of novelty assumes, that it is boring. Boredom is the result of addiction, the first signs of withdrawal. The unexceptional allows the infinitely interesting nature of reality, its eternal freshness, to appear within everything, through every passing moment. This is why we so often remember the small things and forget the momentarily big things.

Holiness is a matter of changing your outlook radically and permanently. Altered states of consciousness lack ultimate interest because they are just that, altered. What is seriously interesting is the changeless. What doesn't make news is the news that matters. Perhaps this is what Jesus meant by drawing our attention to the poor of the world, the persecuted, those whose rights are denied, and those who are denied the front seats at church or the theatre.

If we can pay attention to them, we pay attention to what rarely makes the headlines in the realms of our fantasy-world: the poverty within ourselves. The poverty that is our deepest and truest identity, and where we are most radically dependent on the gift of Being itself. Dietrich Bonhoeffer once said that Christ did not come to call us to a new religion but to a different way of life. It was the life of participating in the weakness of God in the world. This was Mother Teresa's meaning. Participating in the divine weakness in humanity became her habituated state. Her whole way of life. If we are all addicts of something, this was her addiction. No wonder she was so cheerful in the midst of the suffering that broke open her heart. She had found God there.

Usually our habits of mind are different. We are habituated to our anxieties, our work-patterns, our plans, and our fantasies. Every time we sit to meditate, we face these strongly-engrained habits. They form our distractions. They become our escape from the work we know we need to do to be free from them. There are a hundred good reasons every morning and evening why we should skip our meditation. Some of these reasons may be religious ones. It takes time and the faith which expresses itself through the thick and thin of time to establish the habit of meditation. Until it is well-set, the habit of meditation will frequently be broken. Any pressure in life can disrupt the rhythm of meditation and daily prayer: the car breaking down, a problem at work, suddenly realising it is later than you thought, a crisis in the family, the recurrence of an emotional pattern. Once a pattern is broken, it then requires renewed effort to reinstate it.

I recently visited a very beautiful and remote ancient monastery in southern France. The small community of Benedictine monks had returned there about ten years ago and were rebuilding the stones and the rhythm of prayer which had made the place holy over many centuries. Visitors toil up a long and difficult road to visit and pray with the monks whose lives follow an apparently uneventful rhythm, romantic to the visitor, poor to those who practise it. Like meditation, the monastic life does not attract serious news reports. What is really significant about the spiritual journey is not the stuff of headlines, but the "life hidden with Christ in God." as St Paul describes it. Yet this community were sponsoring a serious reflection with many economic and social leaders on the ethics of business and politics. The habits of their life did not allow them a lot of free time. No one can do everything. But their rhythm of life does open up a wide view of life at large and a clear understanding of the meaning of what is there to be seen.

There are different kinds of monasteries and different kinds of good habits of prayer. The life of the monks of Cockfosters running a busy parish and spirituality centre. Or the life of the monks at San Miniato in Florence worshipping daily in an ancient and beautiful place of prayer. Or the small lay community praying regularly together at the London meditation centre, welcoming guests, teaching meditation. These forms of life are not, in the end, ideological. They correspond to the needs and weaknesses of the individuals who live them out as faithfully as they can. Holiness is always particular rather than general. Different forms of life suit different people, and people themselves change over the years and often need to adjust or change their way of life to suit the way they have grown. What all these valuable ways of life have in common, however, is a commitment to regular practise. Through that commitment, the ultimate reality, which contains and perfects them all, can at times be glimpsed. At all times, it is served. And the reality of God is better understood when we approach it in terms of service rather than as something to be grasped as an object of *gnosis*.

Places and communities of prayer—small groups of meditators, for example—are of indispensable value to society. No society can be healthy without this monastic dimension of regular prayer lived out as a witness in its midst. And often a witness made on the edges of society has the greatest impact on its way of life, just as peripheral vision is often the sharpest. If these communities dedicated to the spiritual rhythms of life know what they are there for—for the experience lived in faith and not for show, for liberation from compulsion through freely chosen good habits of life—their social nonproductivity is justifiable. They contribute to the well-being of the world in other ways. Their example is contagious when it is well-lived. People whose way of life is different realise that they too can make a spiritual rhythm of that life. Meditation, lectio, worship—just as St Benedict said a millennium and a half ago. The religious observance which institutional religion bewails as abandoned in this society would recover very quickly if this interior spiritual rhythm were re-established. It makes sense to go to church every Sunday, even if you had a late Saturday, even if the priest is boring, even if your in-laws are coming to lunch, once you see that it is a good habit which strengthens and nourishes the inner life.

Jung said that before we can do what we want, we must learn to do what we don't want. Acquiring good habits usually means identifying and uprooting bad ones. Discipline also requires support and community if it is not to become either fanatical or lukewarm. Good intentions as we all know cool down very quickly. The mind is quick to turn the tables of intention on us, playing games with our perception of reality. Before long, when difficulties begin, the ego's deep instinct to produce consoling illusions is activated. With these false consolations, it throws veils over reality, and these illusions themselves bear the seeds of later habits of self-deception. It is virtually impossible to be clear about all this on our own. Without the wise counsel and loving friendship of others, their authenticity proven by their spirit of forgiveness, we sink ever deeper into the mind's games. If this meant that we thought less, it would not be so harmful, but the more our self-knowledge slips away, the more comforting illusions we produce and the more convinced we become that we are right and others are wrong. This is the breeding-ground of the worst of all forms of the shadow in the spiritual journey: false humility and the illusion of holiness.

The humble know that they are humble—and have a long way to go still before they are fully humble. But the falsely humble will play the game of pretending that they think that they are not humble and that the ill they do to themselves and to others is done consciously. If this sounds complicated, it is because it is complicated. Nothing shows so clearly the simple importance of meditation—praying without thought—as a way to true holiness. The inherent complexity of thought can only be simplified by a rigorous silence and stillness of mental activity.

Complication is the smoke-screen of the pseudo-holy. Religious systems tend always to greater complexity and legalism. The truly humble, by contrast, are not always easy to spot. They don't usually take the headlines or sit in the best seats. This is because they don't much care what others think about them, whereas the falsely humble are constantly exercised by the esteem in which they are held by the world.

> I do not look to people for honour. But with you it is different, as I know well, for you have no love of God in you. I have come accredited by my father, and you have no welcome for me; if another comes self-accredited you will welcome him. How can you have faith so long as you receive honour from one another and care nothing for the honour that comes from him who alone is God? (Jn 4:41–44)

St Benedict warns his monks in the chapter on the "tools of good works" not to wish to be called holy before one truly is. The irony, of course, is that by the time one is truly holy, one will no longer want to be called holy. Or anything for that matter. As long as we are concerned that people should pay us honour, think and speak well of us, we have a good test of the fact that we are still a way off. And there are few of us who do not like to be well-thought of. Few of us like to have our names demeaned rightly or wrongly. Few of us are like the desert fathers who saw advantage in being accused unfairly, as this gave them the opportunity to love their enemies and protected them from the far worse spiritual danger of pride and of luxuriating in other people's good opinions of them.

We grow in holiness by caring for "the honour that comes from the one who alone is God." To care is to love, to turn toward. The honour that comes from God is the dignity of our true nature, our essential and inalienable goodness that makes all of us, in the end, forgivable. To care for this means to immerse ourselves in the holiness of the one who alone is holy. Each time we return to the spiritual rhythm of life in which the image returns to its originating source, we are strengthened in holiness. The whole of creation shows the beauty and power of this rhythm. The sun has the good habit of going down and rising. The body knows when it needs food and drink and how much. Nothing that is not opposed to nature is unholy. Our daily rhythm of prayer partakes in the holiness of nature and its creative source.

With much love

Laurence

Laurence Freeman, OSB

Letter Nine

30 December 1997
John Main's Anniversary

Love in Prison

Dearest friends,

You are probably familiar by now with the WCCM, the World Community for Christian Meditation. I was recently privileged to make contact with what might be seen as a sister community: the WCCW, the Washington Correctional Centre for Women in Seattle. For some time now, Chris Cotton and a small group of meditators have been facilitating a meditation group in this women's prison every Thursday. They do so with great love and dedication, this year even going to meditate with the women on the American Thanksgiving— the equivalent for the rest of the Western world of Christmas Day.

During my visit to the United States in November, I visited this prison to celebrate their weekly mass in the chapel and, afterward, to talk and meditate with the regular meditation group. Prisons are strange worlds, places of paradox, full of surprises. To get in as a visitor, you undergo a security clearance and a thorough physical search similar to the rite of initiation the prisoners are subjected to when they arrive. For the prisoners, however, it symbolises a terrible baptism, a stripping off of the old self and an induction into a new community with new clothes, new language, new timetable. It is a kind of desacralised, mirror image of a monastery. One of the sharpest paradoxes of a prison is, therefore, precisely the discovery of the sacred and the human in so dehumanising and unholy an institution.

We ate a self-service dinner in the refectory, and one could see the surrogate family groupings that form among the women in their isolation from the normal world. For most of them, the path to prison began in a dysfunctional home and often pursued a typical pattern of abuse and neglect. One could see that at least here, as society's outcasts, some of them could find in one way or another friendship, love, and a kind of emotional security. The poverty of their situation is extreme. Perhaps one reason why visitors and social workers feel blessed and humbled by their contact with the prison and its inmates is the selfish reason that it puts their own problems and complaints about life in perspective. Yet, there is also a kind of nobility in the shame to which the women are subjected. It is the honouring of the truth. There is much to regret in the world of the prison, much disfiguring of the human being, for example, through exploitation and drugs. But there is little of the pretence and pretentiousness that characterise so much of respectable life in the outside world.

Perhaps the bottom-line honesty of the life, very familiar to the recovering alcoholic, accounts for the spiritual potential of prison life. I was warned before mass, however, that many women would come just because it was an opportunity to meet each other in a less impersonal setting. That did not seem to me such a bad reason to come. I was also told to keep my eye on the minute hand of the clock because at 6:20 the guard would call muster, and the chapel would empty immediately. But once we started, I was shocked not by the irreverence but by the wave of love and praise by which the mass was borne along. As I simply could not imagine saying any-thing prepared or from on high, I surrendered with them to the work the Spirit was doing in the sacred ritual in that unsacred place. A woman from Alabama called "Country," who has served six of a nine year sentence, sang the country and western music that expressed their own leadership of the service. I was moved by her caring authority for the other women, her spirit of service, and her hard-won genuineness. I have shared in few Eucharists that so clearly taught me why we celebrate mass.

After muster, many of the women returned for the meditation group. Again I was warned that they would be anxious and physi-cally restless and, in a way, they were, but I was more amazed at their degree of attention and stillness during the silence of the meditation and the sharpness of their emotional antennae during the talk and discussion. Clearly what meditation meant to them was what it meant to John Main and every other serious seeker. They had few layers of social identity to protect them from that "naked awareness of the self" to which meditation brings us. The very things that made meditation so difficult for them were also what made it so relevant and so clearly valuable.

For those women in the WCCW and for meditators in the WCCM and for all meditators in every tradition, sitting to meditate is the taking up of the tools of the spiritual craft. Immediately as one begins to say the mantra, the mind puts its agenda on the table like an over-zealous secretary. The hidden agenda is usually felt to be hard at work also. First of all, there are the problems to be solved, big and small. In a prison, a monastery, a family, a job, there will always be problems. Even when things go right for a while and everyone seems happy, that soon becomes a problem because someone will imagine a problem or anxiously wonder how long the peace and good order will last. The mind constantly uses all the changing situations of life to give form to its insubstantial and constant anxieties. And every meditation takes place in a particular life-situation. The dream of a place where you will be untouched by life's problems and can dedicate yourself, without material or emotional distraction, to the "spiritual path" may be worth pursuing, but one should never forget it is a dream: "My kingdom is not of this world." When peace of this kind is found in a problem-free environment, it is by grace as much as by good management.

The desire to solve problems is the first great obstacle to meditation. You have to be clear that meditation is not the time to solve them. Some encouragement can be gained by considering that you are going to the common root of all the problems and their power to upset you. By refusing to be diverted by your anxieties and plans, by saying the mantra with faith and love, you are exposing your fundamental, insubstantial anxiety to the healing peace of Christ which is the gift beyond the mind. How you deal with real insights, on the rare occasions they may dawn on you, will reveal how seriously you are committed to this work and your skill at handling the tools of the spiritual craft. Insights are often accompanied by the dangerous sense that we have successfully solved a problem or, at least, by a feeling of having a welcome holiday from them. In that case, especially when they carry the illusion that you have understood God and solved that problem too, insights occurring during the meditation period should be let go as quickly as the problems which they are illuminating.

In not using the time of meditation cost-efficiently by solving problems or seeking insights, it often seems as if we are acting absurdly. We are not using meditation to wallow in our anxieties like a hippopotamus in its river-mud or to solve our problems like an efficient secretary. We are not even pursuing any kind of spiritual knowledge that makes sense to the mind. We choose to act with the full dignity of our freedom, our divine likeness. We stay in the present moment. We slip into it, or so it seems from the perspective of our egoism, by sliding down the shaft of unknowing and walking bravely through the often dark tunnel of poverty and dispossession.

Prisoners who know they are prisoners understand this. So do addiction-sufferers who have admitted their disease or, to use another vocabulary, sinners who have confessed and begun to repent. The big problem lies with the pharisee hidden in every spiritual seeker. This is the interiorised pharisee who denies being a prisoner of his egoism, who only pretends to be repentant in order to prove to himself and others how unsinful he is, who thinks with all the sincerity of the self-deluded that he understands God.

The pharisee generally does not approve of meditation at all. For one thing, it undermines his confidence in judging and sentencing others for their mistakes and for their good. The mind in general and the ego in particular protest at the choice the meditator makes for the freedom of the present moment. The mind complains it is being neglected or starved. Mind and ego will throw tantrums. If that does not interrupt the meditation, the mind will suggest that we think about thoughtlessness or imagine the formless and then whisper in our inner ear that we have reached silence. All this complicated nonsense shows how serious and simple we must be about the discipline.

Experience, as John Main taught, is what meditation is about—a pure experience which transforms us simply because we are not trying to experience the experience. We are not diluting its purity by examining and using it. Christian meditation responds to the gospel teaching that this experience, the kingdom of God, is within us. The experience that the ego is interested in seeking, however, is neither within nor outside us. It is non-existent except as a mental projection. The kingdom, as Jesus told the pharisees, cannot be observed. But that is precisely what the egotistical mind wants to do: to observe and judge. The spiritual masters remind us that the experience of arrival, of realisation, and of the knowledge of God can be verified only (as Cassian said) because it can be neither described nor remembered.

So why bother to pursue it? Why put so much into the work for something we cannot possess ? The answer is not to pursue it. Not to try so hard. On the other hand, we should also, as someone once remarked, come to meditation with the attitude of a person whose house is on fire! Our life does depend on it.

Meditation for us today is complicated by the cultural attitudes we bring to the experience, indeed to all experience. We look at all experience firstly in the light of our autobiography: what it means and does for me as an individual. The important experiences in life, however, illustrate that this egotistical judgment of what happens to me is mostly illusory. A parent is concerned about what happens for the sake of the child. A husband or wife, friend or partner cannot be true to those life-giving identities without understanding the meaning of their experience from the point of view of the ones they love, not just from their own. So why should we suddenly become so egotistical when it comes to our spiritual experience?

The Christian contemplative tradition teaches us to approach the experience of God in a spirit of othercentredness. Jesus squarely placed the love of God in the same experience as the love of our friends and enemies. This is why meditation has the effect of, in the first place, making us more other-centred—because it is, by nature, other-centred. Our approach to meditation is often based on the illusion that the experience it offers us is private and self-contained. What a wonderful escape from the problems of life meditation would be if it were.

But in fact, the "experience of meditation," like all spiritual experience, translates immediately into a way of life. Those who experience the Resurrection of Jesus in their lives were originally called "followers of the way." So all spiritual practise invisibly and spontaneously translates into the practise of love in every moment, in every thought, word, deed, and movement of the will. The experience then is only meaningfully autobiographical in the context of others. This is much easier to understand when we meditate within a tradition and when that tradition has taken the form of a living community in our lives. This is what meditating in a prison can show you.

We would find meditation less difficult from day one if we could get this clear. But over time, the faithful practise itself will make it obvious. We will see it clarifying in many ways. One of the most central ways it becomes clear will be the way we realise that my problems may be more worrying to me than the problems of others; but they are not in fact bigger or more important. So why do I feel them so much more painfully than the suffering of others? Why do my problems, which are often so much smaller than others, block me from helping them with theirs? It is not long before meditation helps us to see the uncomfortable answer to these questions.

As this becomes clearer in the light of the spirit, we learn to "see" the Body of Christ in its eternal pulsation of universal compassion. We see Christ suffering with all the sufferings of humanity, uniquely with every individual, sharing the burden of every problem, great and small. Does this immediately solve the problems of life? Of course not. But it opens our mind to see that at the centre of the suffering of the world is heart-breaking joy. This may be the solution after all.

For many people, it feels as if their problems are visited upon them by God or the devil. The devil loose in the world is human self-hatred. If we were merely to harm ourselves, it would not be so bad. But we turn this self-hatred outward on others. Politically, socially, and emotionally, we vent our inner anguish on others by scapegoating or demonising them. Society's attitude toward criminal offenders and prisoners testifies to this. The habit of self-hatred and its displacement onto others is so strong and unconscious, it requires a deep and faithful spiritual practise to uproot it. Little by little, as we deepen our contemplative practise, however, the anger and hatred which fill the world are converted—at least, in our little part of the world—into the miracle of forgiveness and love.

Happiness and misery seem to chase each other round the wheel of life. If you were to stop people in the street and ask them if they were happy and what made them happy, most would start thinking about their relationships. Jesus made it clear what his priorities were, too, by leaving the single command that we love one another. Yet for some reason, we tend to separate our human relationships and our spirituality, our love of God and love of each other, as if they were incompatible. Sometimes they are even seen in opposition to each other—as in the religious person with no capacity for human affection or the dedicated carer for others who denies the reality of God.

Meditation opens an experience of how deeply integrated these two dimensions of our human reality are. We try to separate God and other people because we are separated from our true selves. As long as the deep original sin of self-alienation stays unhealed in us, we will suffer from the anxiety of separation. In the distance between the ego and the true self rage the storms of grief and anger. While this distance feels so real, we will also feel separated from God, from ourselves, and even from those we love.

This is why the first level at which meditation is felt to be working is our relationship with ourselves. At first, this is difficult. Meditation allows no self-deception. We see ourselves as we are. It is impossible to avoid seeing the ways in which we are phony or hypocritical; our illusions, self-deceptions, fearful insecurities, and compulsions stand out clearly; and the way we judge and dismiss others so arrogantly will strike a dagger in our conscience when we see it. By facing this dark side of ourselves, we enlighten it. We see it with a light that shines from somewhere deeper in ourselves. And this light of our spirit burns away our self-hatred with the ultimately unavoidable and revolutionary truth that we are good and lovable.

The more conscious of the true self we are, the more we see our attitude to others change in the way we live out our relationship with them. Fear diminishes, generous love grows; reactive anger yields to the wisdom of forgiveness; judgementalism is absorbed by patience. In place of the control and manipulation which, in the ego's eyes, makes the world go round, an amazing freedom is glimpsed as a real possibility in human affairs: the freedom that arises when people let each other be who they are. The world would not be perfect even if we did that from childhood on, but we would need far fewer prisons, and those in prison might be the ones who would benefit from being there.

But what a risk! The great risk we take in meditation is first of all to be ourselves. This is the first step. If we did not take the corresponding next step, we would never move from where we are; we would be hopping on one leg all our life. The next step is to take the risk of letting others be themselves. Perceiving their reality as distinct from our own is the way to do this. And to see them as real is to love them. Iris Murdoch once wrote that "love is the perception of the individual." She went on,

> Love is the extremely difficult realisation that something other than ourselves is real. Love, and so art and morals, is the discovery of reality. What stuns us into a realisation of our supersensible destiny is unutterable particularity.

Turning attention away from ourselves toward the greater reality "outside us" that contains us is the great act of contemplation. It is the same act of contemplation however we manage to do it—in relationships, in art, in service and duty, and in prayer. Certainly, learning to meditate—a lifelong art to learn—is a fundamental way to do it. But it is not limited to the actual work of meditation. To meditate is to learn how to live contemplatively in everything we do. St Antony of the desert once called his disciples to him and told them to "always breathe Christ."

Small things hold great mysteries. William Blake spoke of the holiness of the *minute particular*. Meditation as a daily spiritual practise soon becomes a way of life in which our attention to small things expands the horizon of our perception and the richness of our existence. Discretion—the great virtue of the desert tradition—grows in our judgment and dealings with others. With discretion comes the wisdom of balance and moderation. A strong compensatory force is needed to correct a life that has swung out of balance and is veering from one extreme, one crisis, to another. Discretion, as a spiritual fruit of meditation, is an extremely powerful force capable of doing this. It keeps us centred in the midst of storms and tragedies. We learn eventually not to give up meditation when life's problems get too difficult. We learn that you can meditate even in prison when it seems your life has stopped. We come to feel the effect of meditation in all the difficult experiences with which life confronts us: how to deal with troubles of the heart (falling in love, falling out of love), how to cope with jealousy or greed (in yourself or others), how to live with a thorn in your flesh.

The contemplative mentality, which meditation cultivates gradually, becomes our habitual style of life. This will not diminish our energy or love of life. In fact, it will energise us and make life seem even more wonderful. The vast amount of energy we can expend in coming to simple decisions, for example, is reduced. The problems which occupy us do so for less time. The anguish of choosing dissolves in the act of attention. When we look clearly and truly see, we learn the efficiency and delight of attentive waiting. What we should do shows itself with less of the distorting effort of our will.

John Main's life and teaching, which we celebrated at the International Centre of the World Community today, testifies to this contemplative vision of life as strongly now as it did when he died fifteen years ago. His insight into the communal experience at the heart of meditation is bearing rich fruit in the community of meditators and their relationship with other groups and traditions. His heroically simple teaching on the discipline of meditation itself continues to challenge and to guide countless individuals and small groups in prisons, homes, churches, hospitals, both to begin and to persevere. His balance and discretion remind us where to look and where not to look for the fruits.

When I spoke to the prisoners in Seattle, I reflected back to them what their eyes told me and what John Main has taught so many— that the most important thing is to open your heart to love. To those who are wounded and frightened, this may seem an impossible hope. To those who have been rejected by their families and by society it may seem they are even unworthy to hope for it. But as we are all wounded and fearful of reality, we all have to have faith, at least in the possibility of hoping. This is what meditation allows to happen and why it is such a great and important gift to share. One of the ironies of life is that the most open hearts are found in the most unlikely places. Perhaps that is why Jesus pointed us toward them as places where we would find him:

For when I was hungry, you gave me food; when thirsty you gave me drink; when I was a stranger you took me into your home, when naked you clothed me; when I was ill you came to my help, when in prison you visited me.

As the new year begins, let us keep each other in our heart so that we can be more generously empowered to make this vision a reality in our lives and in the life of our community and the world.

With much love

Laurence

Laurence Freeman, OSB

Letter Ten

21 March 1998
St Benedict's Day

Holy Land

(Editor's Note: The following letter is comprised of journal entries made during the Community's pilrgimage to the Holy Land.)

Dearest friends,

Thursday

February 27. Arrive at Gatwick Airport about 6:30 A.M. Too early to feel very spiritual about the pilgrimage to the Holy Land, especially on learning that all seats were pre-assigned, and I am assigned a middle seat. It all seems rather unclear. But as more familiar faces from Ireland, Canada, the States, Argentina, Singapore, and England appear into bleary view near the check-in counter, a warmth and hope begin to stir. When I see Gordon and Daphne, veterans of many Monte Oliveto retreats and seminars, smiling and chatting with old friends and making new ones in their easy friendly way, a positive sense of community begins to stir: the impersonality of the airport, its duty-free frenzy, and early morning hamburger eaters is what now seems unreal. . . .

As the coach pulls out of its bay at Tel Aviv, a frightened looking woman runs from the terminal with her bag, almost left behind. Irritability is looming. Michael, our guide, is Israeli but born in Stratford-on-Avon, an erudite archaeologist with a prickly academic personality, and we wonder if we are going to like him. The pilgrimage has started, as irreversible as life. We are all in the same bus together, in a lulled rather than wakeful silence. It carries us through the night and through the Tel Aviv traffic. After dinner at the hotel in Tiberias, we gather to meditate in a room set aside for us near the front door. Pat, having organised many meditation retreats in Florida, has thought to bring a colourful Tibetan cloth and candle for the table. An unseen hand has also placed a single carnation on the table. I have my portable gong. These few symbols help to create a sense of the sacred as buses rev up outside and the front desk of the hotel buzzes with activity. However tired and grubby, it feels a relief to meditate. The silence, despite the noise around, is deep and trusting. There seems a purpose in our being together to form a community on the road. After meditation, we begin to feel more at home with each other as strangers cross the room to introduce themselves. On my way to my room, I see Michael entertaining his new charges at the bar. Asked why he came to Israel, he replies that here is the only place a Jew, even a non-religious one like himself, can feel normal and at home. Religious or not, we all need to feel at home. In new surroundings, you realise that feeling at home boils down to being with those you are happy to be with.

The pilgrimage had seemed threatened by the latest Iraqi crisis, and there is still a slight feeling of danger: how troubled and violent this holy land has been for millennia and how much suffering has been inflicted on other human beings in the name of religion. Maybe our hybrid global community, meditating here in the silence all religions revere and forget, will not be useless. If, on retreat, we explore the sacredness of time, finding the present moment of God in the passing hours, on pilgrimage, our attention is focused on space. In these places of ancient and holy memory, maybe we will sense God to be closer than we can imagine. If the body cannot lie, maybe the earth here in the land of the Incarnation will also tell us truth of the *shekinah*: the presence of God.

The next morning, the sun rises red over the Sea of Galilee. After meditation, we listen to the story of Jesus calming the Storm on the same sea two thousand years ago. And, we are told later, storms still whip up out of nowhere and, in minutes, turn the calm lake into a dangerous rage.

Friday

On the Mount of Beatitudes, the octagonal church represents the eight happinesses of Jesus' great sermon, each a facet of the Kingdom whose centre is here and everywhere. We gather and read the Beatitudes, and the words sound in some new resonance with the place. The green hillsides sloping down to the harp-shaped lake are sprinkled with blood-red anemones. These, probably, are the "lilies of the field" of the King James translation and, whether they are in fact the flowers Jesus meant, they really are clothed in splendour. Like the poppies on the old battle-fields of Flanders, they have a painfully simple beauty. We walk slowly down the stony path to Tabga. I see Gordon and Daphne holding hands to steady each other on the steep bits.

Annoyance as some end up in the wrong church, but after running to and fro, we are gathered again at the site on the lakeside where Jesus liked to withdraw to for silence and solitude. A Benedictine community of nuns prays here and cares for pilgrims, and an efficient Filipina nun with a twinkle in her eye helps us prepare for mass by the lake under a canopy of branches. I have left my habit in the coach, and it is a long walk back to the sacristy, so she tells me to let nature be my stole.

The sunlight sparkles cheerfully on the water in millions of dots of light. The carpet of light makes the water look very walkable. We read the Feeding of the Five Thousand, and the generosity it extols seems easy and natural here at this moment. Why should we not share all we have when we have in fact received so much? It is the feeling that we do not have enough or that even we ourselves are somehow inadequate that deceives us and tricks us into meanness of spirit, third-world debts, and poverty-traps. And because we do not take time simply to be, to see, and to relish the bountifulness of life, we become too scared to share, too cynical to be thankful. As we walk by the lake after mass and meditation, someone tells me of his mother's recent death and how its occasion healed a hostility that had simmered for years. When we are peaceful, we can see death in life, fearless in the clarity of this sparkling light.

After a lunch of St Peter's Fish, a couple of us go on our own in search of a Byzantine church but end up lost in a garbage dump.

Finding our way back, we visit a rather Indian-feeling shrine to the wife of an uneducated rabbi whose determination to make the best of him turned him into a great spiritual teacher. We return to the lakeside, and I fall into a deep grateful sleep. As I awake, a large fish jumps in the quiet lake—perhaps the reason I wake. I miss seeing it, but I hear it and see the ripples. As we approach the hotel for our evening meditation, the Sabbath service in the nearby synagogue has begun, and we stop to listen to the lively pleasing chant reaching us through the open windows and watch the chatty coming and going of the congregation.

Saturday

A golden Sabbath dawn over the Lake. After meditation, we read the gospel of Jesus' visit to Nazareth and his rejection by his townsfolk. His family thought he was mad. Perhaps they asked him why didn't he come home and start a nice healing practise there and bring benefit to his own instead of wandering around making trouble with the pharisees and with nowhere to lay his head? We know little of Jesus' personality or psychology but much more of how people reacted to him.

At Capernaum, we see the excavated remains of Peter's house. It is uninspiring, especially after Michael tells us with relish of the academic rivalries among the competing archeologists. We go to these sites not because "x marks the spot" of an event but to commemorate it. In commemorating, as in the Eucharist, what happened once happens again, here and now. In the small synagogue though, where Jesus unrolled the scrolls of the law and taught, there is a sense of presence. We sprawl on the stone benches to rest, casually at ease with it. Up to the Golan Heights and as we pass the military camps and burned out Syrian tanks, Michael tells us that Israel is a peace-loving country: "It loves a piece of this and a piece of that." The theatre of war suddenly becomes comic, a way of dealing with its horrors. Humour is one of the Jews' best weapons. We forget how much Jesus must have laughed.

This is Druze country: a gnostic religion with such a tradition of secrecy that most of its adherents do not know what they believe. They hold that there is a finite number of finite souls who are constantly reincarnated. No explanation is offered for increasing population. Who, someone asks, are the soul-less ones? Near us where we celebrate mass in the grounds of Caesarea Philippi, beside the grotto of Pan, we are close to the Druzes celebrating boisterous family sabbath picnics untroubled, it seems, by non-belief or the soul's non-existence. This spot used to be thought the source of the Jordan, but modern research says there are multiple sources. It would be easier to write and believe, "This is the source of the Jordan." Life is full of might-have-beens and almosts. They keep us tolerant and protect us from extremism. Too many certainties make us dangerous.

It was here that Jesus asked his disciples who they thought he was. When we are not watching our footing on the path, we think of that as we walk beside the fast-flowing Jordan, distracted by the many shards of thousand-year-old terracotta pottery in the ground. This is the same road Jesus walked from Capernaum, allowing him plenty of time to think and talk with his companions. And for some of us in his footsteps, it allows us time to sketch the abundant wild-flowers and view of the Crusader castle over toward Mount Hermon. The English clamber to the cliffedge, delightedly naming the flowers to each other. By the waterfall ("Israel's Niagara") we are involuntarily baptised in the spray.

Whoever we say Jesus is, if we give ourselves time to listen to his question, being here changes the way we respond to it. Faith is stimulated by the emotion of presence here. The magical names and legendary places acquire a geographical scale and relativity. Jesus is given a context we can physically share and a historical time to which we can, to some degree, relate. His presence in the risen state and his historical presence through memory feel as if they are woven together. Having a guide who has no vested interest in making the places fit the stories actually makes this context even more fecund. Presence is the important value on pilgrimage, not measurability or proof. One can always deny a given proof, but not a felt presence. Nor is it only in the "sacred places" either that the presence is found. In the coach and at dinner, there is the same presence. It is perceptible in a group that is so palpably at ease with each other, nationality and social background being merely sources of curiosity, in the marriages like the Mackenzies that have endured the events of half a century, in the silence of meditation we unquestioningly share and slip easily in and out of together—and, though he might be annoyed should we say so, also in our non-religious guide.

Sunday

Ominous weather. The gospel readings after meditation anticipate the places we will visit: Mount Tabor of the Transfiguration, Cana of the wedding feast, and Nazareth. The sublime and the ordinary. . . . We dismount from the coach and pile into the waiting Mercedes taxis to make the winding ascent of Tabor. One of the Bedouin drivers tells us he used to take the pilgrims up by camel. "Now," he says patting the steering wheel, "we have German camels!" Michael regrets that the weather has lost us the view. As I come to the altar wearing my habit and stole, everyone stands up respectfully, and I notice how they had taken the distant pews rather than the benches around the altar. The intimacy we were sharing must have seemed wrong in a big church. But we quickly recover the forgotten peace and gather around the altar. As we listen to the gospel of the Transfiguration, we hear nothing about the view but we are told of the "bright cloud" that enveloped Jesus and the disciples. And so, even the bad weather is good news. I remember the Dalai Lama's reading of this gospel at the Good Heart Seminar and how he never doubted its factuality. No Tibetan would doubt that the body can become light. The light of God which raised Jesus from the dead shone in him in life as well. But what does it mean unless the same light is in us waiting to make us radiant?

At Megiddo, one of Solomon's fortified northern cities on the plain of Armageddon, the weather turns suitably nastier. The greatest number of battles in the ancient world were fought here, and it is here that biblical fundamentalists expect the final conflict between good and evil to happen. The atmosphere of the place has a kind of innocence and neutrality; perhaps having witnessed so much bloodshed, it knows how pointless it is to fight over land that no one can own forever. An ancient temple here from 3000 B.C. used to keep a fire continuously burning. If your fire went out at home, you had only to walk over to the temple to rekindle it.

Perhaps remembering the effect of the church's architecture on our communal spirit on Tabor, someone reflects how easily that religious service might have become a means of control by denying people access to the fire or imposing conditions on it. Thunder begins to roll, and we run for shelter in the underground water-supply system. As we descend the steps into the tunnel, someone whispers that they are claustrophobic, pauses, then adds only half-jokingly, "I seem to have so many phobias, actually."

Nazareth lives up to Philip's disparaging judgment on it in St John's Gospel—"Can anything good come from Nazareth?" I take a photo of a dismal, drizzly street, which for ugliness rivals the strip of any big city of the world. The church here unfortunately took its cue from the town, and we, especially the English, I am ashamed to say, indulge our pilgrims' shadow-side by irreverently laughing at the awful mosaics of Mary. The quiet centre of all the bad art is the house of the holy family (which Michael quietly remarks looks suspiciously like a second-century tomb).

Here, however, there is also a still point of presence and the floor marker says that *"Hic Verbum caro factum est"*—here the Word was made flesh. I realise it is true: if this was Mary's home, it was here Gabriel appeared and she uttered her *fiat* and conceived. I remember the beautiful Pontormo *Annunciation* in a church in Florence where Mary is walking upstairs and, between two steps, has her attention drawn to the angel's sudden appearance behind her. It is the moment of sheer surprise before she begins to understand anything of its meaning: the sublime intersecting with the ordinary in a moment in time. The shabby ugliness of Nazareth, on the way back to the bus, seems more meaningful now. Feeling so like the places we ignore at home, it makes me aware of the need to make every day a pilgrimage, even the routine days we commute to and from work, and to find the presence everywhere.

After dinner, we go out on a boat on Lake Galilee. In the middle, the engine is turned off and we are quite still. The gentle waves are sinuous as if forming something like a body, but the water is dark and reminds one of the closeness of death. The presence here seems strong but serious, almost stern. Does it remind us we should not ask like spoiled children for more signs, more proof? We have been given just what we need. But it is not easy: to see the body of light forming in the current, we must be immersed in the waters of darkness.

Monday

A few miles from Jerusalem, we visit Abu Gosh, "the" site of Emmaus and an unspoiled Crusader church, now the home of a community of Olivetan monks and nuns. A shy young monk gives an increasingly self-confident talk in the church and then flees. We break bread and meditate among the perfect acoustics of the bare medieval walls.

The evening meditation is not so atmospheric. The new hotel is more luxurious, to our pleasant surprise, but less efficient, as we were not given the room to meditate that we were promised. We do so anyway in the dining room amid the clatter of the waiters' laying the breakfast tables. The reading from John Main, not to worry about distractions in meditation, is well-chosen. As we press on undeterred into the silence, doing nothing, the waiters gradually become quieter. And, however distracted our meditation may be, their work seems to become more mindful. Several of our group on leaving remark what a deep silence we had shared. The hotel television, someone else remarks, has twenty-nine channels.

Tuesday

At the wailing wall, we are greeted by dozens of Japanese supporters of Israel, the women in kimonos and the men in business suits, dancing in circles and singing Zionist songs. Then they march off sharply to the mosque in single file. Monty Python does not seem far away.

We celebrate mass in St Jerome's tiny cave in Bethlehem where he lived many years and translated the bible into Latin. He chose this place for his work for the same reason we have come here—because the gospel told us about it: if the Word became flesh, in the gospels the Flesh becomes word. Being here in the historical sources of our tradition, one feels a new intimacy and equality of faith with the great saints who have bowed here down the ages. The grotto of the Nativity, an historically probable site according to Michael, has a womb-like intimacy. Crowded into its small space, our group feels like a representative of all the humanity reborn here. We are not sure how to express the emotion of the experience. So we form a circle and in turn each of us speaks aloud our name. . . .

Wednesday

In a closed garden of Gethsemani on the Mount of Olives, we celebrate early mass. We face the city that has risen and died so many times in history and that Jesus wept over just before his death. Between us and the city walls, there is the Kedron valley that he walked across after the Last Supper. After communion, we disperse around the garden to meditate, some sitting under the olive trees. Here, too, there are the red anemones we saw on the Mount of Beatitudes and everywhere in Galilee. Perhaps Jesus was reminded of home if he saw them here on his last lonely vigil of prayer. Nearby, some of the trees are five hundred years older than Jesus. After meditation, we quietly assemble near the entrance to an old rock tomb similar to the one where Jesus must have been laid, except there are still bones in this one. We read of his meeting with Mary Magdalene and the unfathomable silence of his presence and of his words in all the ways he showed himself to his disciples. We conclude mass and leave quietly. . . .

Saturday

After breakfast, we gather for a wrap-up session. Emotion is quite deep but not sentimental. Various announcements are made. Gordon speaks with his lovable enthusiasm about the Bed and Med plan he and Daphne thought up and now coordinate. Someone else speaks about the Friends, the newsletter, this year's Italian retreat. Family matters.

At the airport, we are questioned about our trip by security. The answers we supply seem foreign to the experience we have had. The questions are meant to ensure our safety, but they are not the right ones. We meet to meditate in the airport synagogue, a tiny room that makes us feel like forty-eight meditators in a submarine. There is the sense of imminent separation—and so many shared glances and smiles.

As we are boarding from the departure lounge, I am told that Gordon is unwell. When I reach him, Daphne is kneeling beside him, and he is clutching his chest. The airline people are kind and efficient, and we get him to hospital quickly. Two of us stay back with Daphne and accompany her to the hospital and through the following anxious hours of waiting. Eventually we hear the good news that it is angina, not a coronary. Gordon, with his military mustache, is sitting up in the emergency ward beaming his child-like smile that has also such perception in it. He is beginning to recover from the pain and the shock of the attack.

It was not the conclusion to the pilgrimage any of us had imagined, and we are still feeling our way around its meaning, like getting to know a new visitor. Daphne is frightened but very strong. Between them both, as long as I have known them, there has always been a communication of silence, but now it seems amazingly, confidently strong. When they speak, they talk about ordinary practical things but there is a deep and certain shared knowledge between them, and they share more than they can say. We establish Daphne at her hotel and make the necessary calls. Gordon is expected to be sent home in a couple of days and return to London. Over the next few days, we learn that the diagnosis has changed, and he has major surgery but again is said to be recovering. Everyone on the pilgrimage is phoning in to know the latest news.

21 March, St Benedict's Day

I am in Florence with a meeting of group leaders when I learn by phone from London that Gordon died earlier today in the hospital in Tel Aviv. Daphne tells me that in the days after the operation when he seemed to be recovering, he reminisced at length about their life together. Forty-eight years of marriage, one for every one of the pilgrims. They were planning their golden jubilee at the London meditation centre. Perhaps his reminiscing was the remembering that our pilgrimage was about—the kind of remembering that removes the veil of time and makes really present what we think is past. We remember together and are re-membered to one another and to the presence itself, the I AM, in which all is present at once. This sharing of presence deepens the union with those with whom we share it. Like pilgrimage itself. Like the making present of meditation.

The thought of Gordon's absence and Daphne's grief feels, to us who shared the pilgrimage of meditation and the pilgrimage to the Holy Land with them, much like an empty tomb. The symbol of pilgrimage fills it with meaning, however, and does not seem false consolation. Would we have gone to the land where Jesus died unless now he also lives? Gordon, a loving and lovable fellow-pilgrim, has made his pilgrimage, and already through it, he is telling us something about Easter. It is the presence we had felt accompanying us through the peaceful beauty of Galilee and in the anxious muddle of Jerusalem, in the hours of silent meditation, rising up within us as we made merry together at Cana, greeting us in the fast-flowing Jordan and in scarlet wildflowers, on dark still lakes, and at sacred and not-so-sacred sites. This is the presence that feels so strong in the mystery of Gordon's newborn silence.

We all extend our sympathy to Daphne and to hers and Gordon's children, and we wish them the fullest joy of Easter.

With much love

Laurence

Laurence Freeman, OSB

Photos of the Holy Land Pilgrimage may be viewed at the WCCM web site: www.wccm.org.

Letter Eleven

11 June 1998
Feast of Corpus Christi

Wounded Healers

Dearest friends,

Sixty-five meditators from several continents joined recently for a week of silent retreat at LaVerna. This is the mountain of pilgrimage in Tuscany where St Francis of Assisi in 1224, two years before his death, received the stigmata. We spent the night of the first day of travel at the foot of the mountain, and early in the crisp sunny air of the next morning, we walked slowly and in silence up the steep footpath to the sanctuary. At the Chapel of the Birds we paused to listen to the ecstatic birdsong which had greeted Francis and his three companions when the birds flocked around him and joyously reassured him that he had arrived at the right place. He came to make a forty day fast and to prepare for the coming of Sister Death whose quick approach he was already sensing.

As we settled in to the simple Franciscan retreat house and began to feel the atmosphere of this intense and sacred place, we agreed to ask ourselves a simple preliminary question. Why had we come here? Like most simple questions, it was a key that opened many doors. Eventually, in the silence which we were now entering, the question led to those other seminal questions of consciousness and the spiritual life which bring us to the brink of thought and so to the light of God within us: Who am I? Who is God?

The story of Francis's experience of prayer on the holy mountain of LaVerna enriched, challenged, and guided us day by day. We heard how he had moved into ever deeper solitude during his stay, alternately battered by his inner demons and consoled by angelic visitations. He persevered in this until he reached that culminating experience of union with the humanity of Christ that has made this place so sacred, not only to his Franciscan followers but also to the whole Christian tradition of prayer.

On the night of September 14, the Feast of the Holy Cross, his faithful friend and companion, Brother Leo, disobeyed Francis's instructions and stole into the solitude of his hermitage to see how he was. In the moonlight, he saw Francis on his knees in prayer and, in fervour of spirit, repeating aloud the questions at the heart of all prayer—"Who are you my most sweet God. . . . Who am I your unprofitable servant?" "And these same words alone did he repeat and said nothing else," St Bonaventure, his biographer, tells us. Brother Leo watched as fire descended on Francis's head and enveloped him for a long time. When Francis eventually noticed him, Leo asked what was the meaning of all this. Francis replied that he had seen two lights for his soul: the knowledge and understanding of himself and the knowledge and understanding of God. In this prayer of fire, God had asked him for three gifts, and he had searched his poverty until he found a gold ball which he offered three times: the gift of his vows.

Telling Leo not to spy on him any more, Francis turns to the Bible to learn what he is being prepared for, and each time he consults it, he is led to the Passion of Christ. So he returns to prayer in solitude "receiving much sweetness in contemplation." He is then impelled to ask for the grace of feeling, not only the pain of Christ, but the love which had enabled Christ to bear it for us. He began contemplating the Passion with deep devotion until he "altogether transformed himself into Jesus through love and compassion."

In the morning, he saw a seraph approach him in the form of the crucified Jesus. He felt filled simultaneously with fear, joy, wonder, and grief. And he was given the insight that his transformation into the form of Christ would not be achieved by physical suffering but by an "enkindling of the mind"—a transformation of consciousness in love. Yet, the sign of this transformation was the permanent "writing" of Christ's five sacred wounds onto Francis's body. Soon afterward, Francis left LaVerna to return to Assisi to die "with the flame of divine love in his heart and the marks of the Passion in his flesh." He humbly asked his brethren if they felt he should make the stigmata public knowledge and was convinced he should when they told him the experience must have meaning, not only for him but for others.

There were many reactions among us as we listened to this story. What connected them all was a reverent sense of mystery—experience that cannot be adequately explained by reason—and the need to express reverence by seeking the meaning of the experience. The deeper experiences of our own life-stories also demand the same reverence and impel a search for meaning. And meaning does not always yield itself quickly or easily. Not to give the time and the stillness of attention needed to become fully conscious of what we have gone through is a characteristic of our fast and impatient age. Time and attention are needed if we are to avoid treating life superficially. Superficiality squanders the precious sense of the sacred that gives depth and purpose to our often perplexing encounters with intense joy and suffering. Mysteries like these are expensive gifts, time-consuming realities.

First of all, with regard to Francis's experience, we needed to ask what it meant and for whom? For Francis himself, for the church, for us today? Perhaps the meaning for Francis is intimately and inaccessibly his own—this is the solitary meaning of all unique experience. We can suppose from what we know of Francis that his stigmata symbolised a high achievement of the union of his personality with the person of the Risen Christ, the one he loved so constantly and passionately. The mystic's—and the lover's—consuming desire is always to shed their egocentric identity and to unite permanently with the Beloved in a way of being in which I and Thou, while not obliterated, are no longer fixed entities. "I live no longer but Christ lives in me." The chasm of separateness is closed when ego is transcended. "A consummation devoutly to be wished"—yet one whose very fulfillment fills the ego with dread and painful foreboding. Unlike Francis, most of us recurrently withdraw at the very moment our desire for full union is offered its satisfaction.

The life of Francis was an ascending, sometimes spiralling, pilgrimage to this union of his humanity with the humanity of Christ. Unlike his followers who idolised him, Francis saw his life-story filled with frequent failures and the backsliding of his own sinfulness. Like most founders, he died with a sense of failure. At the same time, he was aware of and manifested an ever-deepening joy that was the proof at a deeper level of perception that his growth was constant. The coexistence, the intermingling of joy and suffering, pain and peace, love and loneliness, became with increasing clarity the unifying theme, if not the experience, of our retreat. Even the changing weather during the week expressed this as we passed from days of being hemmed in by damp, cold mist to brilliant days of warm sun and expansive views.

Whatever more the stigmata meant for Francis as the extinction of his separate identity in love, it was also the seal on his vocation and mission in the church. Francis's experience decisively influenced the course of Christian spirituality. His union with Christ at LaVerna begins an epoch and a shift in Christian consciousness. It was left to St Bonaventure—as Francis himself was no theologian—to formulate the devotion to the historical Jesus, particularly that focused on the Cross, which opened a new dimension in Christian thought and feeling.

And what might the stigmata mean to us? We wondered as, day by day, the peculiar intensity of LaVerna invited us to ask ourselves more seriously who God was and who we were. It reminded us of what Francis saw in the great light of his fiery experience, that the knowledge of God and self-knowledge are inseparable and that once they are fused we are changed forever. We wondered what was the "golden ball" of our own lifestyle by which we offer the gift of ourselves to God. We saw that if Francis could feel simultaneously the conflicting emotions of fear, joy, wonder, and grief, we, too, must be prepared to stop clinging to any single dominant mental state which habitually obsesses us—not to identify ourselves with our anger, fear, or desire, for example. And that we must learn to be detached from all our feelings if we are to be thrown open to the mystery of God across the entire range of our humanity. We saw how in his simplicity, Francis illustrates the tragic dimension of life in which joy and suffering are inseparable partners. We questioned our culture's fixation on the pursuit of a happiness that denied our inescapable condition of mortality and woundedness. In the mysterious sign of Francis's union with Christ, we sensed how the desire for union, which is the deepest of all our drives, can only be realized in purity of heart, in wholehearted single-mindedness. Union happens when it is our only desire: when the familiar drama of conflicting desires, which cause us to repeat old patterns of failure, has been radically simplified. As we read of Francis leaving LaVerna, riding a mule because of the pain of his wounds and entering into the last phase of his life as a healer of other's wounds, we understood how no experience which we can identify as an experience is final. We are always moving on. "Angels stand still," a Jewish saying puts it, "the saint is always moving."

Finally, wondering who Francis really was, we saw how he had become a friend of humanity, one of the great Christian *boddhisattvas*. The pope's choice of Assisi as the place for the historic meeting in prayer of religious leaders of all faiths in 1988 was inspired by the universal friendship Francis entered upon. Saints, it seemed to us, are not just to be worshipped as paragons of excellence but approached as friends for the spiritual journey who, in Christlike humility, realise what seems without them an impossible paradox of a universal intimacy.

After his stigmata, Francis was sealed in the living expression of the archetype of the saint, sage, or shaman. But most expressively in the Christian sense, he embodies the wounded healer. Once when Brother Ruffino was touching Francis, he curiously put his hand into the open wound in Francis's side and made him recoil in pain. Like him, we are also inclined sometimes insensitively to invade the private wounds of others—the media today makes a good living out of it. We all know how our deepest wounds can shrill with pain when a thought or a careless word or action touches them.

The sense of touch is a dominant theme in Francis's spiritual life. He is joyously in touch with the material world and its many splendoured beauties. He is constantly shown touching and being touched by human beings and by other creatures. Those who touched him in later life often felt they were healed simply by doing so. His great oddness demonstrates the higher sanity arising from being a little touched by God. His wounds were touches of God that changed him irreversibly.

We are wounded most deeply and painfully not by the accidents that happen to us—however tragic—but by love. As everyone who has suffered knows, all suffering is bearable—or unbearable—in proportion to the degree of love with which we are able to be in touch. Love itself, however, is the greatest wound of which humanity is capable. There is the sweet wound of love that can transform the personality and our powers of perception. It can lift us from a black-and-white, one-dimensional world into a universe of undreamed of colour and ever-changing perspectives. And there is the bitter wound of love when love is withdrawn, when its emotional expression withers, when it is deprived or betrayed. Or when the one we love dies. The emerging theme of the retreat was teaching us to open ourselves to the sweet wound—as Francis was opened to the "joys of contemplation"—and also exposed us to the other cutting edge of the sword of love's reality, the bitter wound and the pain of irremediable loss.

A wound is a rare experience of permanence. Most things that happen do not last. We need, therefore, to distinguish wounds from hurts, the setbacks or disappointments which punctuate life and which can be bitterly painful but which, in time, can even fade from memory: the exam failure, the financial loss, the missed connection. From all these, we recover. Wounds, though, mark us forever and change our deepest chemistry of perception and the very functioning of our identity. A wound means that nothing will ever be the same again. Time mends hurts. It does not heal wounds. Only eternity, immersion in the waters of the present moment of the presence of God, can heal a wound. As the wound of Christ's death could only be healed—in the Resurrection—when he immersed himself in the dark depths of his divinity.

Of course, the feelings and sense of meaning associated with wounds change with time. All meaning is made by reading what we are examining in its context. We cannot see the meaning of Francis's experience on LaVerna outside the context of his own life and that of his historical culture. The meaning of our own wounds—which at first often seem horrifically meaningless—emerges as we live them in relation to the other events and patterns of our lives. If the pain permits us to remain conscious enough to do so. But wounds are never erased, just as an end or a beginning can never be repeated. They are part of our story, and our story, however insignificant an atom in the universe it may appear, is a unique and indispensable part of the way the cosmos is. Our wounds, therefore, are among the most sacred forces that shape our existence and make the world itself what it is.

It is important to avoid sentimentality or over-optimism with regard to our suffering because both of these stifle hope. Being wounded is dangerous. It can cripple or even destroy the personality. It can push us over the edge into despair or embed us in frightened, cynical isolation and involuntary bitterness of spirit. Even worse, and the history of families and nations is full of examples, it can turn us into enemies of humanity, demons filled with rage against God and cruel and savage toward others. "The wound accepted in the world's way," as St Paul tells us, leads to death. In the death-like state, we are drained of all compassion as the Nazi death-camps run by ordinary people, not unlike ourselves, should never cease to remind us; and we can become particularly vengeful to those who are weakest and themselves most wounded. We can become wounded wounders. Or wounded healers. Like Francis and his model, Christ.

Like Chiron in the Greek myth. The son of the god Chronos and the earth nymph Philyra, Chiron had the misfortune to be born a centaur, half human (the upper half of his body) and half horse. When his mother saw him at his birth, she was so revolted that she got herself changed into a linden tree to avoid having to nurse him. Rejection was thus his first wound. But Apollo adopted him (or at least his upper half) and trained him in the perfection of all the arts and learning. Chiron became a great teacher and mentor to many of the greatest heroes, including Hercules himself. One day at a feast with the centaurs, they got out of hand, and Hercules had to fire a poisoned arrow to quell their rampage. By accident, it struck Chiron. Being the child of a god, he was immortal so it could not kill him. But it left him in the bitterest, permanent agony.

His life changed. He was forced to withdraw to a mountain to tend his incurable wound. In this way, Chiron became expert in the healing arts and all the medicinal powers of nature. As those suffering came to him for help, he also grew in caring compassion for them. It was no longer the famous and powerful who came but the poor and neglected. All these, he healed with the power of his newfound knowledge, and they left grateful but wondering why he, the healer, could not heal himself.

Hercules (the healing wounder), in the course of another of his adventures, came across a way out for Chiron. Hercules had convinced Zeus to agree to release Prometheus from his torment, provided an immortal could be found to surrender his immortality and die. Chiron accepted and, in embracing his mortality and dying, said yes to what he was. He embarked on a new kind of heroism and gave up the futile attempt to heal his own wounds, to be his own redeemer. Death held no great attraction or glory, but it contained a deep and dark truth which all the powers of Apollo could not have expressed. He died and, like all mortals, descended into the underworld. He crossed the Styx, the boundary between the consciousness of the living and dead; he paid his coin to the faceless ferryman, crossed the grey Asphodel fields where the dead waiting to be judged twittered like bats; and he stood in judgment before the rulers of Hades. The myth tells us that he remained here for nine obscure days. Then Zeus rescued him from Hades and lifted him up above the earth to place him forever as a constellation in the heavens: a lesson written in the skies for all to read.

Myths, like the parables of Jesus, were written for the person reading them. They portray the truth of universal experience that we live out personally, thereby achieving our destined uniqueness. Deep in the story of our lives there lies the tragic choice to become embittered by our wounds or to become wounded healers. For the saints like Francis, it is a choice they live clearly and without compromise. For most of us, it remains a long half-made, messy decision which encounters much resistance, much denial, many attempts to cling to our supposed immortality. Jesus clarifies it for us when he invites us all—and who is not mortally wounded?—to share in his healing of wounded humanity:

> And as you go, proclaim the message: "The kingdom of Heaven is upon you. Heal the sick, raise the dead, cleanse

lepers, cast out devils. You received without cost; give without charge." (Mt 10:7–8)

Jesus, always aware of his coming death and wounded by rejection and misunderstanding, was known above all to his contemporaries as a healer. His call to his followers to imitate his healing of human suffering bestows the ultimate dignity on the wounded. As long as we think it is only the whole who heal, we subscribe to the cult of power. Our perception of reality will be distorted by the ego's obsessive pursuit of happiness and evasion of suffering.

The secret of Mount LaVerna is, after all, not so esoteric. It opens up a vision of supreme human happiness—the bliss of knowing one's true self and God in the love of Christ. And it is believable because it is also true to the inescapable reality of suffering. Francis's wisdom, the wisdom of Jesus, teaches us that our woundedness is not an impediment to the loving service of others. It is the very condition of our being able to alleviate the suffering of others. As long as we pursue our own happiness as the first priority, we will consciously or otherwise do so at the expense of others' well-being. But if we come to the relief of others' pain, we will find the fullness of being for which we are all created. To heal while we are ourselves wounded is not, however, in the ego's realm of understanding.

No one is worthy of me who does not take up his cross and walk in my footsteps. By gaining his life you will lose it; by losing his life for my sake you will gain it. (Mt 10:39)

The meaning of Francis's experience at LaVerna is best explored in the context of his prayer: just as our own conscious living out of these paradoxes of the spirit will depend upon the depth of our prayer. In Francis's prayer, the emphasis is not essentially on the visions and revelations and miracles that fill his biography. Meditation soon teaches that we do not need them and should not pursue experience in this way. Even for Francis, they were not the substance of his relationship with God as his life in community and his insistence on the supreme values of poverty and humility show. More to the point is his steady perseverance in the deepening of continual prayer. He frequently returned to periods of solitude and deepened a life of contemplation that was sometimes joyful, sometimes intensely difficult.

It was this embracing of the whole spectrum of reality that sensitised him so thoroughly and keenly to the presence and activity of God in everything, in every form of the natural, as his Canticle of the Creatures shows: "Aroused by all things to the love of God . . . in beautiful things he found beauty itself."

Seen in this light, Francis's love of creation and St John of the Cross's emphasis on detachment from all creatures appear as complementary rather than the irreconcilable opposites they may seem. We see detachment in Francis and celebration and praise in John. Wherever truth is lived, opposites coexist. Not only joy and suffering, but even life and death themselves. In seeing this, we know what the woundedness of Christ proclaims—that life is not negated by death but consists in the cycle of death and rebirth. That cycle leads in the fullness of time to the deathless state which Francis once prayed to be given an experience of before his union with Christ on LaVerna:

> And as he continued in this state of mind an angel appeared to him in great glory, holding a viol in his left hand and a bow in his right. While Francis was wondering at this sight the angel drew his bow once across the viol; and immediately Francis heard so sweet a melody that it filled all his soul with rapture and made him insensible to every bodily sensation. As he later told his companions, he doubted whether, if the angel had drawn the bow back again across the viol, his would not have left his body because of the intolerable sweetness. (*Second Consideration of the Holy Stigmata*)

Meditation neither seeks nor rejects such experience. It brings us to the egoless depth in which experience of God is possible beyond all self-conscious desire. We are not seeking mystical plenitude but union in the mystery of love. The meditator must become a wounded healer by faithfully entering this mystery of joy and suffering and rejecting all escapism and false consolation. This fidelity gradually moves the mountain of egotism. It is a sharing in the life of Christ that is his continuous dying and rising within us:

> Wherever we go we carry death with us in our body, the death that Jesus died, so that in this body also life may reveal itself, the life that Jesus lives. (2 Cor 4:10)

As we, too, left LaVerna for the next step of our individual pilgrimages, we did so nourished by the community we had shared
and the truths we had tasted in each other's company. This seemed
to me the power of the community which meditation releases and
for which so many today, often without knowing it, deeply hunger.
May our steady daily practise allow each of us to share in that healing of our world.

With much love

Laurence

Laurence Freeman, OSB

Letter Twelve

21 September 1998

Loving Earthly Beauty

Dearest friends,

After the John Main Seminar and the retreat which followed, I drove down the winding coastal road to the Camaldolese monastery at Big Sur to give a retreat with a group dedicated to the practise of the Jesus Prayer. The weather was gloriously clear, and the wildflowers along the cliffs were resplendent. Sitting on top of one of the highest cliffs, the monastery itself is an oasis of calm— each monk living in a self-contained hermitage, joining with the community for prayer and a daily meal, spending much time in solitude. In the early mornings, one looks down on the clouds that have rolled inshore over the ocean during the night. They remain until about midmorning when the cloud carpet rolls back, and the blue Pacific and its whitecaps are once again revealed.

The people on retreat were seriously contemplative, something which was obvious because they were not too solemn or pious about it. St Diadochus of Photike, an Eastern Father of the fifth century, was also with us through his great work in the *Philokalia*, so we all hoped for a peaceful and enriching weekend, which it turned out to be. I enjoyed sharing the wisdom of Diadochus with the group, their quickness of response and spiritual understanding, my walks along the cliffs, and the prayer with the monks. It was the kind of retreat everyone should be able to experience from time to time away from the world.

On the Sunday morning, however, I was disturbed by a prayer for Northern Ireland that one of the monks made at the end of the Office. It was not detailed but seemed to suggest that another tragedy may have occurred to set back the long hard way to peace. With one thing and another, it was not till I was on the plane that evening heading for Brazil that I was able to hear the terrible details of the bomb at Omagh which killed twenty-eight people, traumatized their families and friends, and shocked and revolted the world. Because we are awash nowadays with "News," it may already seem to have become history—to us at least, if not to the families who must hardly have begun their mourning.

As I flew to South America, I had time to recall the moment at the monastic office when the news first broke on me. The strangeness of the world and its infinite contradictions struck me. How one part of the family could be setting off bombs in a Saturday shopping street to kill people and their children, while another part, on a remote and beautiful mountaintop, peacefully prayed and discussed the spiritual life in order to pray more deeply seemed very strange and problematical.

The dilemma it raises must be as old as Christianity or as the spiritual life itself. Leaving aside the question of the beautiful cloisters of monasteries, what, I asked myself, justifies even the urban lay meditator to search for peace and joy in their spirit through daily practise and periodic times of retreat, while all around them the fury and chaos of the world rage and so much suffering and tragic unfairness burst upon the innocent? The only justification can be that it is a duty, not a right, luxury, or privilege to pray at depth. Whatever time and resources are devoted to our "spiritual life" can only avoid the accusation of selfishness if they serve to bring us closer to the heart of the suffering world. Unless the peace and harmony we find through our spiritual life also gives birth to a compassionate union with the suffering of others, it can claim neither reality nor depth. The unselfish fruit of meditation is simply love. So if there is a goal to our meditation, it is not our own fulfilment. How better to express it than to say that it enables us to find happiness, not by selfishly seeking it but by relieving the suffering of others. This we do best not only by what we *do* but even more deeply by what we *are*. Karl Rahner said the holy person is "one who is aware of the suffering of others." Only be aware.

When I returned from my travels to London, another weekend retreat awaited me, arranged by the Christian Meditation Centre. This time, it was called "Finding God in the Desert of the City" and, rather than a Californian clifftop looking over the Pacific, we were in the stressed and polluted city, and we were not even residential. About a hundred of us moved to a different location each day. Our places of meeting were a lecture room at the Friends Meeting House near Euston station, a church hall with windows looking onto the Hammersmith flyover, a meeting room in an old people's home south of the river. The travelling there took its toll on our peace of mind and mindfulness no doubt. At the end of the day, the peace of our meditation and spiritual conversation and Eucharist together were again put to the test by returning home on public transport or through traffic jams. As I passed the homeless in the storefronts and recognised the suffering of loneliness in the eyes of so many of others passing by, I remembered our old friend Diadochus whom we had read on the clifftop in California. He helped clarify for me again how our personal spiritual journey relates so intimately to the problem of evil and the pain of suffering that surround us.

With a calm clarity that could only have been the fruit of confronting the tendency to evil within himself and of having endured the dark nights of his own spiritual journey, he spoke of "attention." Evil does not exist by nature, he said,

> nor is any one naturally evil, for God made nothing that was not good. When in the desire of his heart someone conceives and gives form to what in reality has no existence then what he desires begins to exist. We should, therefore, turn our attention away from the inclination to evil and concentrate it on the remembrance of God; for good, which does exist by nature, is more powerful than our inclination to evil. ("On Spiritual Knowledge," 3)

Simone Weil, confronting the rampant evil of Nazism that overtook her world fifteen hundred years later, came to the same insight: that attention to the good is the greatest power for exposing the unreality of suffering and thus dissolving its power over our minds and emotions. She, too, recognised the dark tendencies in her own personality and suffered the purifying dis-illusionments of the mind's ascent to truth.

Our consumerist and materialist conditioning preaches to us that we have a right to be happy. We make ourselves and half the world miserable in claiming that right at the expense of others when we see the race for happiness as a competition. The desires of our heart, as Diadochus taught, are formed into images, and those images begin to exist in a half-light of reality. By acting to make those images more substantial, we release the power of illusion into the world through those same egotistical desires. Human beings, who are not naturally evil, can then plant bombs in shopping streets, exploit the poor, deceive the credulous, corrupt the young, betray the beloved. A small but tragic error lies at the core of this unhappy human drama. More than possessing the right to be happy, we are born with a duty to be happy which we fulfil only by discovering the true nature of happiness.

Our education—spiritual and cultural, psychological and physical—should better be oriented to helping us learn with the minimum of mistakes (but enough mistakes to teach us) what makes for true happiness. When I was in Brazil, I participated in a conference on the education of the gifted child and spoke on its spiritual dimension. I learned much from the dedication of the experts in that field and was moved by their sensitivity and awareness that the spiritual dimension means more than another item of a syllabus. It is a vein of awareness that must run through the whole art of teaching and every institution of education. I shared with them the thought that the child is more than human material to be formed for work in the world. The child (and part of us will always be the child we once were) is a symbol of wisdom. To teach a child well, we need to see wisdom within them and help them to treasure it. Growth then awakens in the mature person that treasure hidden within wisdom that is compassion.

Diadochus contemplates human nature and the world from a high vantage point that nurtures the most expansive degree of compassion. Typically contemplative in his outlook, he sees the natural goodness in all, even those who commit evil or waste their lives in foolishness. For Jesus, this all-encompassing compassion—that is proven by our love for those who harm us—is the true nature of God who causes his sun to shine on good and bad alike. But it is also the true nature of our human godlikeness, and Jesus frees us from egotism by telling us to be "perfect as your heavenly father is perfect."

Attention. Awareness. Seeing the goodness of human nature. Contemplative consciousness changes the world. It transforms the cold observer of suffering or one who condescends in pity into one who is truly compassionate. This has immense significance for society, for education of the young, and for the care of the disadvantaged. It leads to a just and peaceful society. It has no less relevance for the church as it painfully struggles into the new form that the Spirit is bringing to birth through its present death and dying. Sometimes today, Christians look at the words and actions of their fellow-disciples and wonder if their institutions have lost the spirit of the gospel altogether: painful condemnation and bitter argument, power struggles and hollow piety, the fear of punishment and exclusion rather than the happy assurance of forgiveness and acceptance. Historically, one might sagely say, this has pretty well always been the case. But contemplatively, as the great saints have said over and over again, it is also simply and always unacceptable. The church may be the "test of our faith as well as an object of faith," but the suffering within the church forces us to seek a deeper meaning of "church." How can we be aware of the true, good nature of the church as a place of reconciliation, not condemnation, as Pope John proclaimed when he launched the current period of renewal? How else but by truly looking, truly seeing with that pure attention which is contemplation and which produces not condemnation but the good judgement born of compassion.

Christians, like the rest of the world, suffer the pain of living amidst a pluralism that lacks consensus. Time was when people argued with each other over definitions of the truth but did so within a common unifying vision of reality. Even when reconciliation among them seemed impossible, there was appeal to at least an external authority. Like children who benefit from boundaries in their training, this gave everyone a sense of security. But now, in the chaos of competitive modern pluralism, we are forced to grow up, to set our own more subtle, interior boundaries marked out by the insights bestowed by wisdom and compassion. Societally and globally, we are painfully learning what a discerning tolerance of different views and practises really means. We learn not to condemn those who disagree with us but instead only to condemn those outrages like Omagh which everyone sees to be inhuman. Of course, there are boundaries and not everything is acceptable. But the most unacceptable, because potentially the most destructive of the happiness and peace of others, is intolerance. The fruit of contemplation is tolerance. The antidote for fundamentalism—which can trick even the most sincere fundamentalist into participating in the abuse of others—prejudice, racism, ageism, homophobia, sexism—is contemplation. Only contemplative consciousness ensures that metanoia, or conversion, does not stagnate and, instead, becomes a continuous and deepening experience of our spirit.

So the call to deeper spiritual experience which is being heard by so many today is not an escape from the dilemmas and responsibilities of these troubled times—even if they are the "beginning of a new dark ages," as some fear. As short-term social and economic solutions seem to fail us with greater frequency, and the brittle facade of our political system lies exposed, what else can we do except "go deeper"? Depth here means spirit. We find the spiritual dimension in those sacred realities of life, common to all, which are the realities of birth and death. These inescapable realities unite us with our fellow human beings in an intense awareness of wisdom and compassion—even with those with whom we may profoundly disagree. Nothing is more natural. Death and birth instinctively move the heart to compassion, to a shared grief and joy. Perhaps this is why the care for the dying is one of the most powerful spiritual movements of our time.

At the end of my trip, I participated with many others in an international congress on palliative care in Montreal, one at which John Main gave his last public talk in 1982. This year, representatives of many spiritual traditions also shared their understanding of human wholeness in the light of the mystery of death and dying. It seemed to me that the Christian insight into wholeness is rooted in the attainment of that vision of God which divinises us, as the ancient Fathers taught. And this vision is born in a heart that has been purified by wisdom through the poverty of suffering and the richness of love. There is no life without death, and no death without suffering, but wisdom empowers us to see that the meaning of suffering is love. It is perhaps the most difficult lesson that our human development has to instruct us in. We reject it when we first sense it because it demands such a re-prioritising of life's values. Yet, it is one we have to accept and embrace even without fully understanding it. The fact that love leads to suffering is not so difficult to understand. It is the stuff of romance. Love leads to a progressive deepening of self-offering, of the death of the ego. We can die into this death of the ego or choose to suspend love and reduce its demand. This we all do. Yet, to love is to embark on an unstoppable journey through continuous stages of self-transcendence. Commitment and fidelity continually deepen; and yet with every deepening of commitment, some less real part of ourselves must be allowed to die. Not surprisingly, we run from the death that love invites us to enter because we cannot or have not yet believed that its suffering will lead to deeper love.

The healing care of the dying is a work of love that demands much from the carer, but it also gives much in return to all those playing their roles in the sacred drama of death. All benefit, all learn, all experience healing because the mystery of the individual's dying is a universal mystery. In this awareness of the unifying power of love and death, in the human fellowship experienced at the moment of death, the Body of Christ is manifested to those with the faith to recognise it. To see this is to see God. Seeing God requires only a pure heart. The best conditions for a good death and for good caring for the dying, therefore, are those which purify the heart. Although the environment and atmosphere are important, it is the interiority of these conditions which really define the spiritual life: stillness and mindfulness, silence and attentiveness, simplicity and empathy. That so many in our society die in hospitals without these qualities being nurtured around them expresses what we have lost and are desperately seeking to recover in our culture: the sense of the sacred lost through our forgetting the practise of contemplation.

The great teacher of this united mystery of love and death is the Cross—the personal cross which every meditator picks up each day and carries into an ever fuller experience of Resurrection. Love and death are the twinned mysteries of life by which we are healed and through which we evolve into transcendent wholeness. Jesus, his life, teaching, death, and Resurrection, incarnates this truth. He does not only utter it. He is the utterance of it. And to know him in this way is to know the Truth. If we see how an ordinary person with all their limitations can sit beside a dying person or hold the hand of a suffering relative and do so in a way that reveals the deeper powers of human wholeness, it is easier for us to glimpse how Jesus does this universally. Whenever we turn toward him in the joys of love or the pains of dying, our personal experience is transformed by union with what is universal in his experience.

When I was at the national forum of the Australian meditation community in Brisbane, I was shown a remarkable painting by a Christian, aboriginal woman artist. It was composed of the rich earth colours and dot patterns which have characterised aborigine art for millennia. I was impressed by it but misunderstood it. I saw it as an abstract composition but was told that it represented the ritual of a tribe in different stages of the cultivation, harvesting, and grinding of their crop of grain. Having been told that, I saw it in a new way. I had been given a new way of perceiving it. I realised that there were two quite different perspectives integrated in the painting. There was the global overview, the bird's-eye view, and also the inward perspective which is only open to those who renounce that observer-status in order to participate. It is the same with our relationship to Christ. We cannot see him as long as we are merely observing him.

There is a surprising moment in Diadochus's treatise "On Spiritual Knowledge" when he is speaking of the obstacles to contemplation. He refers to the loss of our appetite for "earthly beauty," and many would be inclined to think that he is about to say that as we lose this appetite, our taste for spiritual realities will increase. In fact, he says the opposite. If we lose our love of earthly beauty, he says, we will suffer a listlessness and lowering of our capacity for life itself, and so we will soon lose our capacity for spiritual knowledge and growth. He has an essentially Christian understanding of the wholeness of the human person and so of the specific capacity of our body to experience the same delight in the goodness of God as does our spirit. It is this insight into the goodness of our nature and of all reality which teaches the Christian about the universal call to contemplation, whatever our walk of life.

Our city retreat in London clarified this. Like desert monks of old coming together from their cells to share the feast of the inner kingdom, the participants came from all walks of life but shared a very practical sense of the challenges of their spiritual journey. We talked of the challenges of living the contemplative life in a city today: its stresses and distractions, the pollution and noise, the levels of competitive anxiety and the premium on time. But we also understood that these very obstacles to *apatheia*, as the desert tradition called the state of inner calm, are also opportunities. Anyone facing these hindrances to peace every day is made aware of the fundamental need to meditate faithfully morning and evening.

Commitment to a spiritual discipline deepens with the insight into its necessity. Also, the very situations that cause us to lose peace are those which can reinforce it. Little by little, the daily practise and the natural rhythm of meditation sustain our mindfulness through stressful moments and remind us of the freedom we have over our responses. Stuck in a traffic jam on the way to an appointment, we can chose to fret and fume or to accept the unavoidable and employ the time in prayer. Defeated in the rush for a seat on the train or cut off in the race for the supermarket queue, we can vent our anger, bottle it up, or transform it by recalling ourselves to the cell of our heart. Finding we have an unexpected space of time between meetings, we can prevent ourselves from wasting it mindlessly by deciding simply to do nothing. In our planning of holidays or free weekends, we can judge the real meaning of recreation over mere entertainment. In our homes, we can set aside a space to symbolise the sacred dimension which runs through our whole life and each moment of the day. And in the times we give to meditation, we can choose those slots which most truly sacramentalise the centrality and priority of the spirit of prayer.

Even more than usual, the news these days reminds us of the precariousness of our political and economic systems. For most of us, there is a reasonable chance that we will emerge from the present insecurity relatively unscathed, but there are many around the world, not only in Kosovo, for whom these are terrifying and dangerous times. In our meditation, we are not only deepening the peace with which we can face the impermanence of things and the chaos of change, inner and outer. We are also uniting ourselves with all those others who suffer like or, more probably, more than ourselves. The hope for the world is that we learn wisdom from these events. It is the hope we find equally in the experiences of inner peace and of unity with others. If we can apply that wisdom, if we allow the emergent contemplative consciousness of this era full space to expand, we may better come to know the mystery of the goodness of creation—not only from above, objectively, but also from within because of our sharing in the goodness of God who is its source.

With much love

Laurence

Laurence Freeman, OSB

Letter Thirteen

30 December 1998

Common Ground

Dearest friends,

God's self-giving to us is the divine self-emptying love by which we are simultaneously created and healed. And, as Pope John Paul said in his recent great letter, *Faith and Reason*, the prime commitment of Christian thought is the ever deeper understanding of this self-emptying, God's *kenosis*. It is a seamless mystery, immersed in time and history—our own time and personal history as well as the collective history of humanity. We come to know love and serve the eternal God within the painful and perplexing limits of daily lives and our too often self-centred perspectives. Because we are subject to these limitations, we constantly make mistakes, and so we need the continuous correction of human love and the guidance of the Spirit. Repentance and forgiveness, above all, are the salt of humility. They, not pride or defensiveness or competitiveness, create the self-emptying of all true encounters. In the risk of meeting, we release the Spirit in the wonderful miracle of human communication. This awakens the wisdom which is the tasting of truth.

The epiphany moments in life, like the Bodhgaya pilgrimage from which we have just returned, happen when the truth breaks through—like sunshine on a English winter day or like rain on a thirsty land. However long anticipated, these unveilings always come as a surprise. And yet, however dramatic their external form—Christians and Buddhists sitting under the Bodhi Tree where the Buddha was enlightened, listening to the Beatitudes read aloud before meditating together—the true power of such epiphanies wells up from within. We are changed by the power that dwells within us so deeply that it can often seem impossibly beyond us; it feels so transcendent, and yet there is nothing more intimate. It is closer to us than our own ego-sense of self. It is so subtle and yet so all-pervading that it is beyond definition. This power is the presence both of love and wisdom. Meditation makes us conscious of this presence because it makes us more consciously present to it, not as observers, but as sharers in its being. In this awakening, community happens as the sign of a pre-existent communion. It dispels the diabolical illusion of division.

Our community continues to evolve from the contemplative experience in that Christian tradition of prayer of which John Main was one of the great modern recoverers. The central work of this community is to teach and practise meditation in this tradition. As a contemplative community, we try to be good stewards and to do things in good order. We also try to keep things as simple as possible, sometimes because our resources force us to! We are daily reminded of our fragility, human and material. Although our main work is to contribute to the renewal of the contemplative life in the church at large, we have also been led into a multi-faceted encounter between Christian faith and many areas of modern life. Of these, the dialogue with other faiths, especially with Buddhism in the form of our meetings with the Dalai Lama, has become one of the most significant, self-renewing, and enriching.

After "The Good Heart," the 1994 John Main Seminar led by the Dalai Lama, there was a deeply-felt conviction that we had all experienced one of those epiphany moments. Immersed in time, of course, but it felt like an experience that would not fade away in memory as so many do. The passing of time and then the success of the book proved that the model of dialogue which the seminar had been was of an enduring and deepening significance. It became ever clearer that the spirit of friendship, which both the silent meditation and courageous conversation had together engendered, lay at the heart of this very joyful and very serious encounter of faiths. So it was that, at a meeting last year with the Dalai Lama to review the fruits of "The Good Heart," we conceived of "The Way of

Peace." This is a three-year development of the dialogue and will be unfolded through pilgrimage, retreat, and a common social witness. It began this month with the pilgrimage of about 150 Christian meditators from many countries, together with some of their Buddhist friends from those countries. We came to Bodhgaya at the invitation of the Dalai Lama because it is the most sacred site of Buddhism, the place of the Buddha's enlightenment. At the entrance to the great *stupa,* we were welcomed by the Dalai Lama and led by him to the great Bodhi Tree. In meditation with him under its branches and later by sharing the riches of our traditions over three days, we all came to feel a larger meaning and influence in what we were sharing. In reflective mood, it seemed to many of us that this pilgrimage that we were part of, as individuals or as personal representatives of our traditions, was a journey opening up deeper paths into the heart of humanity. It felt so enriching that we did not want it to be restricted to ourselves, and we believed that more people than we could count would benefit from what the Spirit was teaching us.

At the beginning, I asked the Dalai Lama to explain to us the significance of the Bodhi Tree in Buddhist devotion. He explained how, tired of his extreme attempts to realise enlightenment, the thirty-five year old Siddharta Gautama at last came simply to sit in stillness and wakefulness under the Bodhi Tree. His long night in meditation there took him through many universes of the soul. As dawn broke, he came to his all-penetrating insight into the nature of reality, its laws of interdependence, and its path to freedom. Illusion and egotism crumbled, and the light of pure consciousness broke through with all the power of a universal compassion. He was now Buddha, fully and permanently awake. For forty-nine days, he maintained complete silence, convinced that his experience was incommunicable. But he was eventually prevailed upon to teach, and in compassion for the suffering of others, he pointed out the causes of suffering and the path of liberation. He taught the *dharma,* the simple yet demanding way to *nirvana,* beyond the pain created by ignorance and desire. Like all great teachers of humanity, he proclaimed that the way was universal and ever at hand.

We were reminded of this on the first morning of our pilgrimage as the Dalai Lama greeted us and led us to the cushions which had been prepared for us all under its high overarching branches. The shade that moderates the heat of summer is evoked in the sense of "coolness" which is one of the meanings of the deep word *nirvana*. When we were seated in this shade, I thanked the Dalai Lama for his welcome and explained again that we had come not as tourists or diplomats but as friends and pilgrims. As he replied, a leaf from one of the high branches overhead fluttered down and landed in his lap. Seizing the moment, and the leaf, he handed it over to me with a laugh.

After meditation, the pilgrims came up one by one to receive a *mala* or Buddhist rosary from the Dalai Lama. This was his way of welcoming each person individually and of inviting each of us to make our time there truly prayerful. When we had moved to the Root Institute where our conversations were to take place over the next three days, he told me that he preferred an informal approach to these meetings rather than just the exchange of set talks. I was not unprepared for this. But I was reminded of that sense of standing together on a precipice which had flashed through me at the beginning of "The Good Heart," both exciting and frightening. In all human relationships, even between the followers of different religions, formality is safer and more predictable; but it is not by formality that new worlds are discovered. Progress comes down to trust. The trust needed to risk testing the old in the light of the new. To take the risk of trusting to the personal rather than the formal is the condition of all friendship, including the spiritual friendship with other faiths which the Spirit today is calling all our religions to explore.

Over this period, I have been reading the pope's remarkable letter to the Catholic Church, *Faith and Reason,* and have found in it many insights which have helped me to understand better the meanings of our pilgrimage to Bodhgaya. Even the theme of the letter suggests the characteristic differences of emphasis between Buddhist and Christian traditions as well as their complementarity. But above all, I was struck by the pope's appeal to modern people (to philosophers in particular, but he says that the human being is, by nature, a philosopher or lover of wisdom) not to "abandon the passion for ulti-mate truth." Nor, he says, should we lose the eagerness to search for it or the "audacity to forge new paths" in the search. Passion, audac-ity, and new ways of searching for truth—the pope is well aware of the need for the courage to take risks. "It is faith which stirs reason to move beyond all isolation and willingly to run risks," he says, "so that it may attain whatever is beautiful, good, and true." Faith thus becomes the convinced and convincing advocate of reason.

At the opening of our conversation after the first meditation under the Bodhi Tree, the Dalai Lama gave us a truly good and beautiful sign of this daring attitude of openness which permits all real understanding and sincere friendship. He presented us with a rolled *thanka,* a traditional form of religious painting on cloth developed over the centuries as one of the glories of Tibetan art. He asked me as it was being unrolled if I could guess what the theme of it was. I imagined it was one of the traditional Buddhist themes of the genre. Like everyone else, I was quite unprepared for the beautiful Nativity of Christ painted in Tibetan style which was revealed. It drew a gasp and delighted applause from everyone in the room as they strained forward to look at it. The painting was modeled on a fifteenth-century Dutch altarpiece but has been transformed in artistic style and language by the Tibetan art which so powerfully expresses the most subtle ideas of that tradition. It is a movingly beautiful and unique work of art. The traditional ox may look remarkably like a yak and the lute-playing angel like a visiting *bodhisattva.* But as art often is, the *Nativity Thanka* seems an early sign of a maturing friendship respecting uniqueness and celebrating common truths: something new and yet to come, still deep in human consciousness but even now struggling to be born and be known.

The *Nativity Thanka* is simple, as simple and familiar as the Christmas story itself. A week or so later on Christmas Eve, I found myself looking at it from the altar of my monastery in London where it had been put up on one of the walls of the church for midnight mass. The hundreds of people whose attention were drawn to it were struck by its beauty and the quietly powerful meaning it seemed to radiate. It is a precious sign of the gift human beings are to each other when we reverence what is sacred to each other. And even if we cannot fully understand that sacredness, we can always appreciate its beauty.

On Christmas Eve, I was again reminded of the pope's letter and the way it affirms the universality of the human spirit whose basic needs are the same in the most disparate cultures, In particular, he stresses the "duty of Christians now to draw from this rich heritage (of India) the elements compatible with their faith in order to enrich Christian thought." He goes on to say that this dialogue, respecting essential and historical uniqueness, is as true a function of Christian faith today as it has always been. The Church of the future, the pope says, "will judge herself enriched by all that comes from today's engagement with Eastern cultures and will find in this inheritance fresh cues for fruitful dialogue with the cultures which will emerge as humanity moves into the future." The *Nativity Thanka*, which the Dalai Lama presented to the World Community for Christian Meditation, courageously exemplifies this spirit. How can Christians fail to want to be enriched by a culture who sees the richness of our own? The Dalai Lama's personal interest in commissioning the *Nativity Thanka* from the artist monks of his monastery in Dharamsala showed how generously he has always led the way in inter-religious dialogue as well as responded to the initiatives of others, such as the pope's historic invitation to religious leaders to Assisi. If Christians have a duty to be enriched by the sacredness of other traditions, it is good for us to be reminded that our tradition is revered by non-Christians and that the truths we revere can also be contemplated by those who follow another faith.

After the presentation of his amazing gift, the Dalai Lama asked me to start the wheel of our conversation turning, and I did so by reading from the Gospel of John. It was the description of the first meeting between Jesus and two of his first disciples. Advised by John the Baptist of Jesus' identity, they start to follow him. He then turns to them and asks "What are you looking for?" Stunned by the vast simplicity of the question, they can only respond by asking him where he is staying. It is as if they are acknowledging that what they are looking for will be found when they know where he, at his deepest, is dwelling. The word *dwell* is a special one for St John and evokes his emphasis on the unique indwelling of the Father and the Son, the permanent relationship at the heart of the mystery of Jesus and of Jesus with his followers. The teacher, who teaches most powerfully by asking the questions that awaken the self, now gives them not a mere answer to their question but an invitation: "Come and see," he replies.

It is a story with little action and great meaning. The zen abbot from San Francisco, Norman Fischer, later remarked how struck he had been by the simplicity of the story and its strange precise conclusion: "It was four in the afternoon." For the Dalai Lama, it was the starting point for the discussion of "Enlightenment and Salvation," the twin themes we had chosen for the dialogue sessions of the pilgrimage. This, he began by saying, is after all what every human being is looking for with varying degrees of awareness. In this first session and later each day with a panel of Christians and Buddhists, we discussed some of the different meanings and interpretations of these two great religious ideas of our traditions. At times, the conversation ascended to rather dizzy heights and became finely analytical and rather difficult but then, as the philosopher Wittgenstein once put it, we returned with laughter to renew wisdom in the green valleys of foolishness.

Our dialogue illustrated some of the joys and difficulties of the human thirst for truth, and the fact that no system of thought, however sophisticated, can, as an intellectual system, contain the whole truth. "We can know Him by love but by thought never," as *The Cloud of Unknowing* puts it. We also learned that the similarities between traditions are rightly attractive but should not seduce us into ignoring the universes of difference which it would take light-years to cross. Or which can only be crossed perhaps in the Spirit itself, timeless and unifying. In the meditation periods which punctuated our days, we went even further than sharing a sense of the common human destiny which unites us all. Yet each meditation prepared for a deeper, more trusting sharing. Paradoxically, silence renews the power of words, and stillness of mind clarifies thought.

Meditation allowed us better to see what the pope in his letter calls that "body of knowledge which can be judged a kind of spiritual heritage of humanity . . . shared in some measure by all." In silence, we touch that boundary which is the humbling and wise limit of mental enquiry but which does not invalidate the mind's attempt to understand and question. Truly to touch this boundary demands that we have done our best with all the powers of the mind to push it further: that we have been honest and sincere in our way of speaking with each other and listening to each other. Silence is all the more revelatory when we have respected each others' attempts to say the unsayable, tried to be clear and simple in articulating the truth, and finally acknowledged our limitations. Dialogue brings us to humility as the womb of wisdom. In trying for the impossible, vision comes as purely as any gift.

Only at the limits of our powers of thought does meaning reach its defining moment When it is clear that we are not just pursuing an intellectual game, that we are not trying to be cleverer than the next person; that we are not using ideas to dominate or bully or defend our position or institution; but that we are driven on by the love of truth and the thirst for enlightenment and then salvation, the love of truth transforms into the truth of love, and the need for enlightenment becomes its bestowal. This model of dialogue is not restricted to religious encounters. It illuminates the nature of all human relationship—the way families, lovers, and friends as well as traditions and cultures live with their differences and grow in mutual understanding.

At our limits, we are all poor in spirit, and if we dwell there long enough, we discover our need for God. No one has ever escaped being brought to these limits. The human weakness which St Paul identified as the crucible of divine power unveils itself to everyone whether through old age, sickness and death, emotional loss, failure, or tragedy. Part of the Christian wonder is to contemplate the child Jesus and see the revelation that in this individual God has become weak, the fullness of being has emptied itself, and the boundless has become limited. Such truths awaken humanity beyond its pain and despair. It is not then as intellectuals that we try to make meaning out of pain, but as human beings desperate for the hope only truth offers. And because life is not all pain, we try with the wisdom of humility, not as saints but as compassionate human beings, to embrace and enjoy the pleasures of life without harming others and without selfish delusion.

The spirit among the participants at the Bodhgaya pilgrimage was deeply moving because of the vital connection we sensed between humility and wisdom, very evident especially in the genuineness of the Dalai Lama's humanity. Some of us had traveled together across India. But we all converged in Bodhgaya with a sense of communion with many other members of our community keeping watch with us around the world. As pilgrims, we got to know each other as equals.

It is hard to be a hero to others at 3 A.M. on an Indian train. We worked together to get the administration of the event running smoothly. Such work demands generosity and teaches forgiveness. What we learned from the Dalai Lama and from each other might be said to be the final message of the pilgrimage: how friendship is the great teacher and sustainer of the human quest. We saw how noble and how fragile friendship is. How easily wounded or destroyed by selfishness. How easily attacked by negative forces. Yet it is more than a solace. It is not just a means to self-fulfillment. In the rare and brief glimpses of true friendship, the risk taken of sincerely loving one another, we touch the goal itself. We dwell for a while in the elusive truth and know that at heart we always do. For the Christian, this is what it means to see God.

In the experience of wisdom and compassion that we call truth, the Buddhist "mind" and the Christian "heart" are seen to be one. In hearts purified of selfishness and minds cleansed of attachment, the vision of God is the experience that dwells in us as we in it. It is the experience that can never become a memory because when known, it is known as an ever-present and self-renewing power in the human spirit. Long after the conversations and the explanations, the imagined breakthroughs and definitions have receded or been forgotten, the truth of the friendship that is God remains. The Dalai Lama's probing questions about Christian belief reminded us that this experience of the vision of God does not mean seeing God as a mental object. As the most ancient theological insights of the church affirm—and this guided our conversations at many turning-points—we cannot know God as an object, but only by sharing through grace in God's own self-knowledge. For the Christian, this is the key to the meaning of the baby in the *Nativity Thanka*: all human beings are called to this vision of God because, in the Christian vision, "God became Man so that Man might become God."

Under the Bodhi Tree the following morning, I read aloud the Beatitudes, the eightfold path of Jesus' teaching. They are not directly translatable into Buddhist thought, but I would guess that no one meditating together that fresh morning failed to feel that they were life-giving words spoken from the same body of spiritual knowledge from which the enlightenment of the Buddha flowed. After meditation, the Dalai Lama led us barefoot around the *stupa*, reminding us in this Buddhist devotional practise of how the Buddha touched the earth after his enlightenment to call it to witness to what had dawned in him. Wherever enlightenment dawns in an individual, all humanity becomes more conscious and the earth itself more sacred. When we returned to the meeting hall, we listened to St Matthew's account of the death of Jesus on the Cross. The Bodhi Tree of enlightenment seemed to ask to be seen along with the tree of salvation. Our conversation turned to the meaning and nature of enlightenment. We see expressed in the Cross, in the light of the Resurrection, the Christian meaning of compassionate love and suffering. But what many also saw more clearly through our conversation with the Dalai Lama was that in Jesus on the Cross, we see the clarity and power of his enlightenment, his universal union with humanity. It is seen in his forgiveness of his enemies and his undimmed consciousness of the relationship with his Father into whose hands at last he committed his spirit

Our dialogue was not intended to reach conclusions but to deepen mutual understanding, to generate friendship. One of the ways this happens is by the simple though not easy method of really listening freshly to the questions the other asks you about your own beliefs. When the Dalai Lama asked about the nature of Jesus' enlightenment, what it meant to call him the Son of God, or about the meaning of humanity sharing in the divine nature, the Christian pilgrim is challenged to a deeper clarity about his or her faith. And thus, faith is not weakened or diluted (as the fearful think) by the sharing of it or the risk involved in sharing it. Faith can only deepen and mature in dialogue and through the attempt to share it. Why else does Jesus ask so many questions? When people asked the Dalai Lama about reincarnation, karma, or the present state of the Buddha, I think Buddhists were in their turn also challenged and clarified. Because we trusted each other and friendship was genuine, we were prudent but blessedly free from fear. The fear of dialogue is the virus that breeds intolerance and ultimately unleashes verbal or physical violence against those different from us.

When someone asked what was the real use of our pilgrimage, our meditating under the Bodhi Tree, or our discussing these themes, it made us all think. How, Santikaro, the American Buddhist monk from Thailand asked, would this practically affect our way of dealing with the overwhelming challenge the visitor meets at each step with the thousands of beggars on the streets of India?

We speak a lot each day. Today especially, the technology of communication accelerates and multiplies our conversations to an often deafening and confusing pitch. And in much talking, as St Benedict warns, it is not easy to avoid sin. The more we talk, the more likely we are to forget the subtle meaning of words and the more likely we are to grab at cheap truths, sound bites rather than teachings of the Spirit. The more we lose the silence of truth, the more likely we are to prefer entertainment to instruction. The purpose of dialogue, at least as I understood it at Bodhgaya, is to bring us to the limits of the mind, to that precipice where words reveal their meaning even as they fall over into the silence where communication stops because communion happens. But as we passed from meditation to dialogue, from delicious meals to beautiful prayer, from light laughter to hard thinking, we learned again how many dimensions make up the purity of truth. And among them, both reason and faith are necessary companions on the pilgrimage to truth

Our pilgrimage to Bodhgaya gave us a taste of the first fruits of that new friendship between religions which must be the defining characteristic of the next millennium. What struck many of us so clearly is that religion is not redundant, despite many attempts to destroy it. If Soviet communism failed in Eastern Europe, China will also fail in Tibet. In fact, it has already failed because by its attempt to kill Tibet, its great spiritual heritage has been shared with the world. So despite the mockery and misrepresentation of religion by the media; despite the shallow consumerism that is attempting to replace church and sangha with earthly paradises bought at the expense of the poor; despite the claims of scientism to replace the myth of God, human beings remain essentially religious. The crisis of religion today, especially in the West, is purifying all religious institutions. With its social masks stripped away, it is immediately obvious when religions betray their founders' beliefs and intentions by competing with or condemning each other. The goal of all religion is the perfection of the human being as a person of love and wisdom. It is mocked by religious pride and exclusivism: whether the imperialism of the fundamentalist Christian or the superiority of the born-again Buddhist. Why then be a

Christian or a Buddhist, a Muslim, Jew, Hindu, Sikh, Jain, B'Hai, Zoroastrian. . . ? What does it mean to be a true disciple and follower of one path? Perhaps, this is the essential question with which to enter the new millennium. It is the question which most deftly liberates religion from its own ego. Courageously pondered, it empowers us to love our own tradition with fidelity and obedience but, at the same time, to love our neighbours as themselves.

As the Dalai Lama frequently remarks, he does not foresee or desire a universal religion. The world's religions will no doubt be changed and greatly purified by their meeting in friendship, dialogue, and meditation. But they will not be melted down. However, perhaps a global *spirituality* is a desirable possibility and even a need for the new era. A spirituality grows in silence through the personal inner work of meditation. Religion without spirituality, as the past thousand years have often shown, wreaks disaster on humanity. And so, whoever wishes to remain truly religious and serve the world must discover the contemplative dimension of their own tradition. Once they begin to do so, they find that this dimension is both wholly unique and universal. It is the only true bridge between religions. Bridges allow both sides to remain true to their own identity, while uniting them and allowing free commerce. In the Christian vision, the supreme bridge is the Spirit, at the heart of the Trinity and between God and humanity. This is the Holy Spirit Jesus promised to send as the fulfillment of his mission. His prayer for unity is the mission of the church.

No one saw this more clearly in our own time than John Main. I brought to Bodhgaya the simple cross he was wearing when he and the Dalai Lama met in 1980, meditated together, and shared their views and experiences—a memory still fresh for the Dalai Lama and to which he referred at our first morning session at the *stupa*. The cross acquired the nature of an ancient Irish pilgrim's cross, strengthening many others to follow the new paths which the Way continuously opens up. Today, December 30, the anniversary of his death, the auspicious meeting of Fr John and the Dalai Lama appears to me as the first step of the pilgrimage which brought members of the World Community from five continents to the Bodhi Tree. Today, Christian meditators around the world are meeting and meditating to give thanks for the gift he brought to their pilgrimages of faith. Each week this gift is expressed as they meet in small groups in churches, homes, prisons, hospices, offices, schools, and hospitals to learn to be one with Christ, with themselves, with each other, with all.

Today at the International Centre, we will meet to listen to one of John Main's teachings on tape, to reflect together on the richness of the tradition he passed on, to celebrate the Eucharist, and to meditate together. His tapes continue to astound and enrich me as they do countless others. Like our dialogue at Bodhgayad, they invite everybody to listen, but they do not seem ordinary talks. His words yield new insights and dispel more obscurity on each hearing. And if one were to ask how this is, I could venture two explanations. Firstly, the deep silences that often open up between the words as if making way for the self-communicating experience of the Spirit. To pay attention to the words of a true teacher is to listen and then, never knowing quite how, to find oneself emptied of thought in a full, loving silence. And secondly, Fr John's teaching carries the light that he found in Jesus, the essence of the Christian meaning of enlightenment

The only thing that Jesus destroys are the walls of division. "With the richness of salvation wrought by Christ," the pope writes, "the walls separating the different cultures collapsed." Thus "faith's encounter with different cultures has created something new." The Christian's duty and delight is to accept and explore this new way of being free from divisions. Perhaps the approach of the millennium is showing how we are just beginning to do so.

Only as pilgrims free to roam can we taste the liberty of enlightenment and the pure generosity of the healing we call salvation. Yet all traditions teach that enlightenment requires a path, and a rule of life is needed to set us free.

The path of enlightenment involves sincerely held beliefs into which we can surrender our fears and doubts but without relinquishing the right or the need to question what we believe. Fidelity to our path diminishes the ego. Enlightenment dawns as the ego sets. Fear and desire yield to the intoxicating freedom to love those who believe differently from ourselves and even those who cause us suffering. The ultimate weapon of nonviolence replaces vengeance. The whole human person is changed. We taste the universal in ourselves and surrender ourselves to God. The conflict of opposites becomes the experience of transcendence, which is not a momentary event, but unfolds in a new way and vision of life. It is all unobservable, but it can be recognised as soon as we allow ourselves to be known. We can see it in people of every faith.

We can serve this great vision even before it is fully realised in our individual selves because we are more than individuals. Our great traditions teach us that they are communions of saints and that we belong to them. That our greatest resources are not material or technological but spiritual. The great teachers and lovers of humanity heal the wounds of sin and division. This is what we contemplated as pilgrims, aware of our individual limitations and collective potential, as we all sat in friendship under the Bodhi Tree and watched the leaf of enlightenment fall. The tree of Eden, the tree of Enlightenment, the tree of the Cross. No longer divided. Each bearing its proper fruit in due season.

As we begin this last year of the old millennium, may we grow as a community deeper into Christ and into the universal friendship to which he summons us all.

With much love

Laurence

Laurence Freeman, OSB

Chronicle of the Community: 1995–1998

*An Overview of Some of the News
Items in the Quarterly Newsletters*

∽༄༅∼

Letter One: December 1995

The first response to the Friends Program was encouraging with 160 Friends joining. Three new patrons of the Community were announced, the Abbot General of the Olivetan Congregation, Bishop John Sherlock of Canada, and William Johnston SJ. A new worldwide bed and breakfast program for meditators, Bed and Med, was launched. Three meditators started the first group in Kuala Lumpur, and a new group began in Geneva. Canadian meditators took on sponsorship of groups in poorer countries. Talks were given at San Miniato in Florence and in Rome. The Canadian National Conference was held in Winnipeg with talks on the environment and therapy. In the United States, Laurence Freeman gave retreats at the Benedictine monastery at Pecos, the Episcopal cathedral in Washington, D.C., the United Nations in New York, and the chaplaincies at Princeton and Yale. In September, he spent three weeks teaching in Australia. News was received of growth in the groups in Belfast, New Zealand, and Brazil. Mary Morrison, a meditator involved in the first meditation centre John Main started, died in London.

Letter Two: March 1996

Peter Ng, the director of the Singapore Centre, reported on the community's work there and in Malaysia, Indonesia, and Mauritius. Two meditators from Perth, Australia, spoke on meditation in Sri Lanka. Fr William Johnston SJ traveled in Ireland, giving talks arranged by the Christian meditation community there. A hermit sister sent a message to meditators worldwide saying she did not find it easy most of the time either. Paul Harris criss-crossed Canada, and in Thailand, Emilie Ketudat led a day for Christians and Buddhists.

Letter Three: June 1996

The London Centre in Campden Hill Road celebrated its tenth anniversary. Groups were flourishing in Wales. Giovanni Felicioni gave his performance piece, "The Hairy Christ," in London and led a week's meditation and yoga retreat in Somerset. Elizabeth West taught meditation in Zimbabwe and South Africa. Fr Joe Pereira in India described his integration of meditation and yoga in his recovery program for recovering drug addicts and alcoholics. Laurence Freeman gave retreats in Texas, Florida, and New Jersey and talks in Montreal, Ottawa, and Quebec city. Paul Harris toured Ireland in April. He and Fr Laurence spoke in Belfast where Sr Evelyn McDevitt leads a growing number of meditation groups. Fr Laurence led a retreat in Cork, Ireland in June, and spoke in Belgium and Holland. A group started, led by Catherine Charriere, at San Miniato in Florence. A Guiding Board meeting took place in Princeton, New Jersey, and the School for Teachers of Meditation was discussed.

Letter Four: September 1996

Raimon Panikkar led the John Main Seminar in Ascot, England, on "The Silence of Life" which was attended by about 250 people. At the end of the seminar, he was presented with the first copy of the just published *The Good Heart*. The Monte Oliveto retreat on "Mindfulness" drew meditators as usual from many countries. Laurence Freeman's *Web of Silence* was published. The Archbishop of Brisbane invited the Community to teach meditation over the next three years in his diocese in preparation for the millennium. News was received from Canada, Australia, and India, and in Malaysia, Serena Woon wrote about the five groups meeting on Penang Island. Paul Harris celebrated his seventieth birthday with meditators in Ottawa. Giovanni Felicioni made his final oblation as an oblate of the congregation of Monte Oliveto and led meditation and yoga with Margaret Rizza at the Darlington International Summer Music School. The Centre at San Miniato in Florence was opened with Catherine Charriere and Giovanni Felicioni as co-directors.

Letter Five: December 1996

The Australian National Forum was held in Sydney in September and passed the executive council role from Victoria to New South Wales. Agnes D'Hooghe in Belgium wrote of the events organised by the Brussels centre there and in Holland. Fr Laurence visited Brazil in November and gave retreats with Sr Eileen O'Hea in Minneapolis and Chicago. He helped with the publicity for *The Good Heart* by speaking at various locations as he gave retreats in California, Texas, New York, and Florida. Fr Gerry Pierse, a missionary home on leave from the Philippines, led retreats in Ireland. Cardinal Margeot from Mauritius invited Peter Ng, whose workshop on meditation he attended in Singapore, to teach there. A new national council was set up for the United States at a meeting in Minneapolis in October with Carla Cooper as national co-ordinator. Great appreciation was shown for Fr Warren and Sr Marian McCarthy, whose centre in Chicago continues its important teaching and networking ministry. Two important new books, Greg Ryan's *The Burning Heart* (an anthology of John Main's key scripture passages) and Paul Harris' *Contemplative Prayer,* were published.

Letter Six: March 1997

In February, Laurence Freeman and Eileen O'Hea visited the Dalai Lama in India and formulated the Way of Peace, a three-year program of pilgrimage, retreat, and cooperation on the work for peace. On behalf of the Community, they undertook to help the Tibetan Nuns Project. Agnes D'Hooghe spoke on meditation to a gathering of novice monks in Belgium. Fr Laurence visited Schotenhof monastic community. Fr Denis Mahony SM from Fiji described the seven meditation groups meeting there. Meetings of group leaders were held in Ireland by Sr Margaret Collier, the national co-ordinator. Clem Sauve from Toronto arrived in London for a year as the International Centre Administrator.

Letter Seven: August 1997

Mary McAleese led the John Main Seminar on "Reconciled Being" in Dublin and, soon after, was the successful candidate in the elections for the President of Ireland. The first School for Teachers was held in Florence with thirty meditators spending ten intensive days of discussion and workshops. Laurence Freeman led the Monte Oliveto retreat on the theme of "Spiritual Friendship." Peter Ng taught meditation at Cardinal Margeot's invitation in Mauritius. Retreats were held in Ireland, India, and Australia. The Canadian National Conference was held at the University of Victoria in British Colombia Laurence Freeman led retreats and gave talks in New York, Florida, and California. Medio Media published the first five of its "Retreat With . . ." series. A new look for the Community's web page (www.wccm.org) was launched by web master Greg Ryan in New Jersey.

Letter Eight: October 1997

Reconciled Being by Mary McAleese was published. Paul Harris visited Australian meditators. Margaret Rizza published her new music composition "The Fountain of Life." Laurence Freeman taught in Paris, Lyons, Provence, Belgium, and Holland. Abbot Vittorino Aldinucci blessed the new meditation centre at San Miniato in Florence, which began to function as a centre for Italy and other European countries. Elizabeth West, the United Kingdom coordinator, helped lead a Buddhist-Christian retreat at Plum Village in France. Sr Barbara Hazzard from the Hesed community in California gave a retreat in Florida.

Letter Nine: December 1997

Laurence Freeman led a silent day at the London Centre to commemorate the fifteenth anniversary of John Main's death. Clem Sauve left his role as International Centre administrator to return to

Toronto and was succeeded by Lucy Chong, also from Toronto. Fr Gerry Pierse gave talks in Malaysia, Irish meditators made a pilgrimage to Glendalough, and a new group began in Paris. In November, Laurence Freeman gave talks and retreats in Texas, New Mexico, and California. He also visited the women's prison in Seattle and Green Gulch Zen monastery in San Francisco. *Reconciled Being* was launched in Dublin, and Paul Harris' book of daily readings by John Main, *Silence and Stillness in Every Season* (Continuum), was published.

Letter Ten: March 1998

The community news items yielded to a descriptive article by Clem Sauve on the constitution and the guiding board of the World Community for Christian Meditation. In Italy, Giovanni Felicioni, Catherine Charriere, and Laurence Freeman led the first Italian retreat at Passignano, a monastery near Florence. Laurence Freeman visited the meditation centres in Singapore, Manila, and Malaysia. The first contemplative pilgrimage organised for Christian meditators spent ten days in the Holy Land. The United Kingdom National Conference took the theme of wholeness with talks by Eileen O'Hea, Giovanni Felicioni, and Laurence Freeman.

Letter Eleven: June 1998

The news items were again shortened to make room for an article describing the purpose and organisation of the trust which is the World Community's financial mechanism. A major event was that after Easter at the London Centre the house on Campden Hill Road, which was the residential home of meditation in Britain for more than ten years, was sold to allow a move to larger premises. Laurence Freeman gave retreats in Montreal and Toronto and talks in San Francisco and Arizona, where a new centre was opened in Phoenix. A School for Teachers was held in the United States. In May, Laurence Freeman led a retreat in Cork and visited Wormwood Scrubs prison in London to meditate with inmates. Joe Doerfer took over as business manager of Medio Media in the United States, and several books by John Main and others, not previously published in the United States, were published there by Continuum.

Letter Twelve: September 1998

Laurence Freeman led the annual silent retreat preceding the John Main Seminar which was held in San Francisco with more than three hundred people from fifteen countries participating. The seminar, led by Thomas Keating on the topic of the contemplative dimension of the gospel, helped deepen the friendship between Contemplative Outreach and The World Community. Fr Laurence attended Australia's National Forum in Brisbane before giving talks in Sydney, Melborne, and Tasmania. He went on to visit with groups in Belgium and Brazil where he gave a talk at a UNESCO conference for educators of gifted students. The Portguese version of the *Coming Home* vido was also launched. He then went on to Ireland for a weekend retreat in Cork organised by Sr Margaret Collier. Elizabeth West and the London Community organised an urban retreat led by Fr Laurence titled "Finding God in the Desert of the City." He led other retreats in Belgium, Brazil, Ireland, England, and the United States. In Sarasota, Florida, Dr Balfour Mount led a retreat on meditation and dying. Milo Coerper was succeeded by Carla Cooper as the Chair of the Guiding Board of The World Community. The first phase of the "Way of Peace" would soon be held in Bodhgaya, India, in December, with meditation and dialogue shared with His Holiness the Dalai Lama. Schools for Teachers of Meditation and retreats were planned for the United States, United Kingdom, Ireland, Germany, Italy, and Portugal.

Letter Thirteen: December 1998

The second phase of the "Way of Peace" took place in the form of a pilgrimage of about two hundred Christian meditators to Bodhgaya in India on December 13–16, where they were greeted by the Dalai Lama, with whom three days of meditation and dialogue were shared. Kathleen Minards, a Canadian oblate and meditator in the community for many years, continued to unite the community world-wide as she faced the final stages of a long struggle with cancer. In Poland, Fr Jan Bereza, a Benedictine monk from Lubin, celebrated with meditators the tenth anniversary of the first Christian meditation group in Poland. There are groups in the main Polish towns like Warsaw, Bialystok, Gdansk, Poznan, and Bzreg, and several of John Main's books are now published in Polish translation. In Singapore, more than two hundred meditators came together for the annual retreat in October which was led by Fr William Menninger on *The Cloud of Unknowing*. Cardinal Jean Margeot from Mauritius participated and visited many groups in Singapore. In Germany, Gunter Meng had shared the teaching of Christian meditation, and in 1999 six regional meetings and a School for Teachers are planned. In October and November, Laurence spoke in New York, participated in the United States School for Teachers in Houston, led a retreat, and gave several talks there and in Austin, including some to health care professionals. The School for Teachers was also held for the first time in the United Kingdom and Ireland.

The World Community for Christian Meditation

Meditation creates community. Since the first Christian Meditation Centre was started by John Main in 1975, a steadily growing community of Christian meditators has spread around the world.

The International Centre in London co-ordinates this world-wide community of meditators. A quarterly newsletter, giving spiritual teaching and reflection, is sent out from London and distributed from a number of national centers, together with local and international news of retreats and other events being held in the world-wide community. An annual John Main Seminar is held.

The International Centre is funded entirely by donations and especially through a Friends of the International Centre programme.

The World Community for Christian Meditation / International Centre / 23 Kensington Square / London W8 5HN / United Kingdom.
Tel: +44 171 937 4679   Fax: +44 171 937 6790
E-mail: wccm@compuserve.com

Web Page

Visit The World Community for Christian Meditation Web site for information, weekly meditation group readings, and discussion at: **www.wccm.org**

Christian Meditation Centre / 1080 West Irving Park Rd / Roselle IL 60172.
Tel/Fax: +1 630 351 2613

John Main Institute / 7315 Brookville Rd. / Chevy Chase / MD 20815.
Tel: +1 301 652 8635   E-Mail: wmcoerp@erols.com

Christian Meditation Centre / 1619 Wight St. / Wall / NJ 07719.
Tel: +1 732 681 6238   Fax: +1 732 280 5999
E-mail: gjryan@aol.com

Christian Meditation Centre / 193 Wilton Road West / Ridgefield / CT 06877.
Tel: +1 203 438 2440   E-mail: Internet:pgulick@mci2OOO.com

The Cornerstone Centre / 1215 East Missouri Ave. / Suite A 100 / Phoenix / AZ 85014-2914.   Tel: +1 602 279 3454   Fax: +1 602 957 3467
E-mail: ecrmjr@woddnet.attnet

Medio Media Ltd.

Medio Media Ltd. is the publishing arm of the World Community for Christian Meditation.

A catalogue of Medio Media's publications—books, audio sets, and videos—is available from:

Medio Media / 15930 N. Oracle Road # 196 / Tucson / AZ 85739.
Tel: +1 800 324 8305   Fax: +1 520 818 2539
Web page: www.mediomedia.com